God's Country
Joshua Pettit

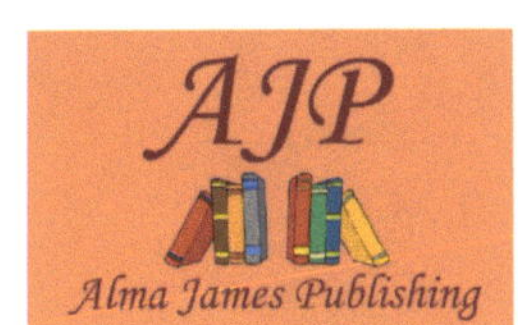

Published by Alma James Publishing LLC
Harrisonburg, Virginia
www.AlmaJamesBooks.com

Published by:
Alma James Publishing, LLC
Harrisonburg, VA 22802
www.almajamesbooks.com

ISBN:

Printed in the United States of America

Foreword

Life isn't easy. For some, though, it seems like it is. They coast through life picking up accolades and rewards, rarely stumbling, rarely struggling. Folks like this sail through their existence, looking good and enjoying the good life.

Joshua Pettit isn't one of those people. Thank God, or else I wouldn't feel like he's someone I could relate to. No, Josh and I relate because we both know what it is to struggle.

Joshua knows struggle. Joshua knows pain. He's constantly dealing with agony in his shoulders which makes it nearly impossible for him tyo find "regular" work.

Joshua and I both lived pout of our vehicles in southern Utah, where heat and dust and the dry desert air are constantly trying to kill you, but where a stunning desert vista awaits around every corner. Every day we saw Zion National Park from our corner of the world, rising in a three-thousand foot sweep of red and white Navajo sandstone to form one of the greatest scenes of geological wonder in the world.

Joshua lives in this setting, and with his sharp eye—forged through difficult circumstances—he captures imaged of the desert and the mountains that reflect the raw and painful reality few understand.

Joshua gets it. He sees. He perceives truth in the creosote bushes and the lizards and the sage. Look more closely, and you will see it, too.

Life isn't easy. The desert is a harsh mistress and a cruel teacher, but she has beauty and lessons to spare. But only if you listen.

You're here now, with this book in your hand. So crack it open, and listen. Maybe you'll get the lessons, too.

Don Gilman
Writer and Videographer
Roseburg, Oregon

Introduction

There's a joke that tells of a reporter doing an article on religion. He goes to Rome and gets an audience with the Pope, and he sees that there's a gold phone on the Pope's desk.

"What's that?" the reporter asks.

The Pope replies, "That's my direct line to God."

"Really!" the reporter marvels. "And how much does a call like that cost?"

"About $10,000 a minute," the Pope says.

Later, the man interviews the Dalai Lama in India, and on the desk is a gold phone.

What's that?" the reporter asks.

The Dalai Lama replies, "That's my direct line to God."

"Really!" the reporter says. "And how much does a call like that cost?"

"About $20,000 a minute."

Finally, the reporter interviews the President of the Mormon Church, and on the desk is a gold phone.

What's that?" the reporter asks.

The man replies, "That's my direct line to God."

"Really!" the reporter says. "And how much does a call like that cost?"

"Nothing. It's a local call."

When I tell that joke to people who've never seen Utah, they often think it's about religion. It isn't. I've traveled a lot. I've seen the Himalayas, and they are magnificent. So are the coast of Maine, the Rockies, Yosemite, and Phi Phi Island off the coast of Thailand. But for sheer beauty, I've seen nothing compares with the high desert of Utah.

It's harsh country. I've often marveled that the early settlers survived. Where I lived in the Parowan Valley, temperatures typically ranged from 110 degrees on a summer day to -30 on winter nights. Most of the precipitation comes in the form of snow. There is a summer "monsoon," but it's unpredictable in timing and volume. Summer is also unpredictable. The last frost may come in March or in June, and the first frost any time between Labor Day and late October.

But what makes it beautiful is the color. Reds, grays, browns, and oranges adorn the hills. A friend from the Midwest said, "It looks like God went wild with a paintbrush!"

And despite the harsh climate, there is a surprising amount of life. From a wide variety of birds and insects, to snakes and lizards, to coyotes and mountain lions, life thrives just out of view. And when the snow melts, the flowers come. Who knew a desert could be so colorful?

There are also surprising things to be found: evidence of human life past, from petroglyphs from a thousand years ago to abandoned foundations and mines of early settlers to lanterns and old cars, you never know what you'll find while wandering the desert.

Joshua Pettit captures the beauty and character of this unique region like no other photographer I've seen. He grew up there, and has lived there most of his life. He has a love for hiking, camping, and exploring. His images capture the not only the beauty of the desert, but its character and contrasts. And in them, one can feel the love he has for this unique place.

I had the privilege of editing this book. I suggested to Josh that his rectangular photos would be more striking if they were cropped to better fit the square pages. But his images are so well-framed that my greatest challenge was deciding which photos could be cropped without compromising their beauty. For some, I just couldn't do it. The framing and composition was too perfect to change.

If I had my way, I'd cover the walls in my house with these images. I love Josh's photos, and I trust that you will, too.

D.J. Mitchell
Author, Publisher, and Pastor

www.DJMitchellAuthor.com

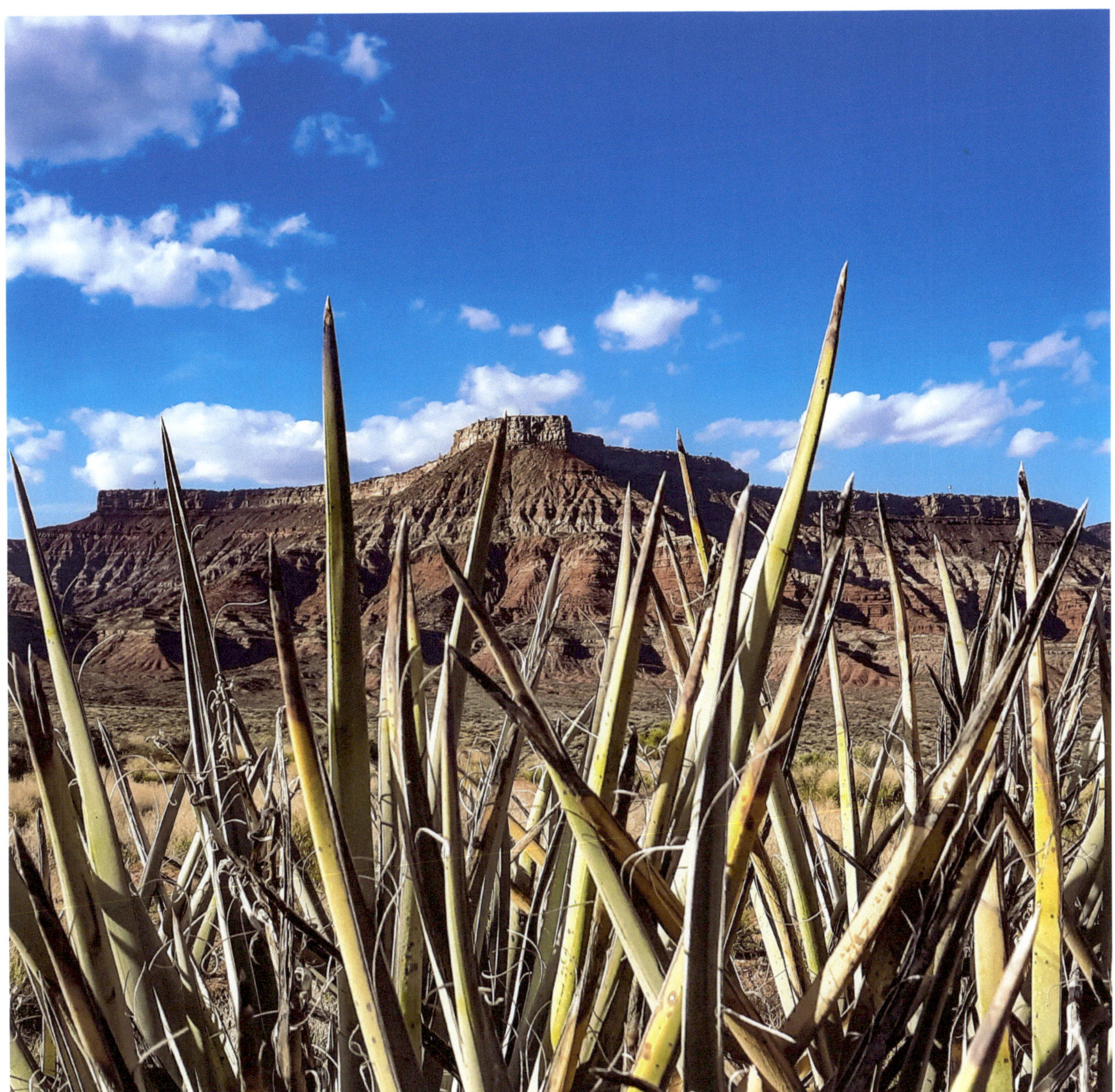

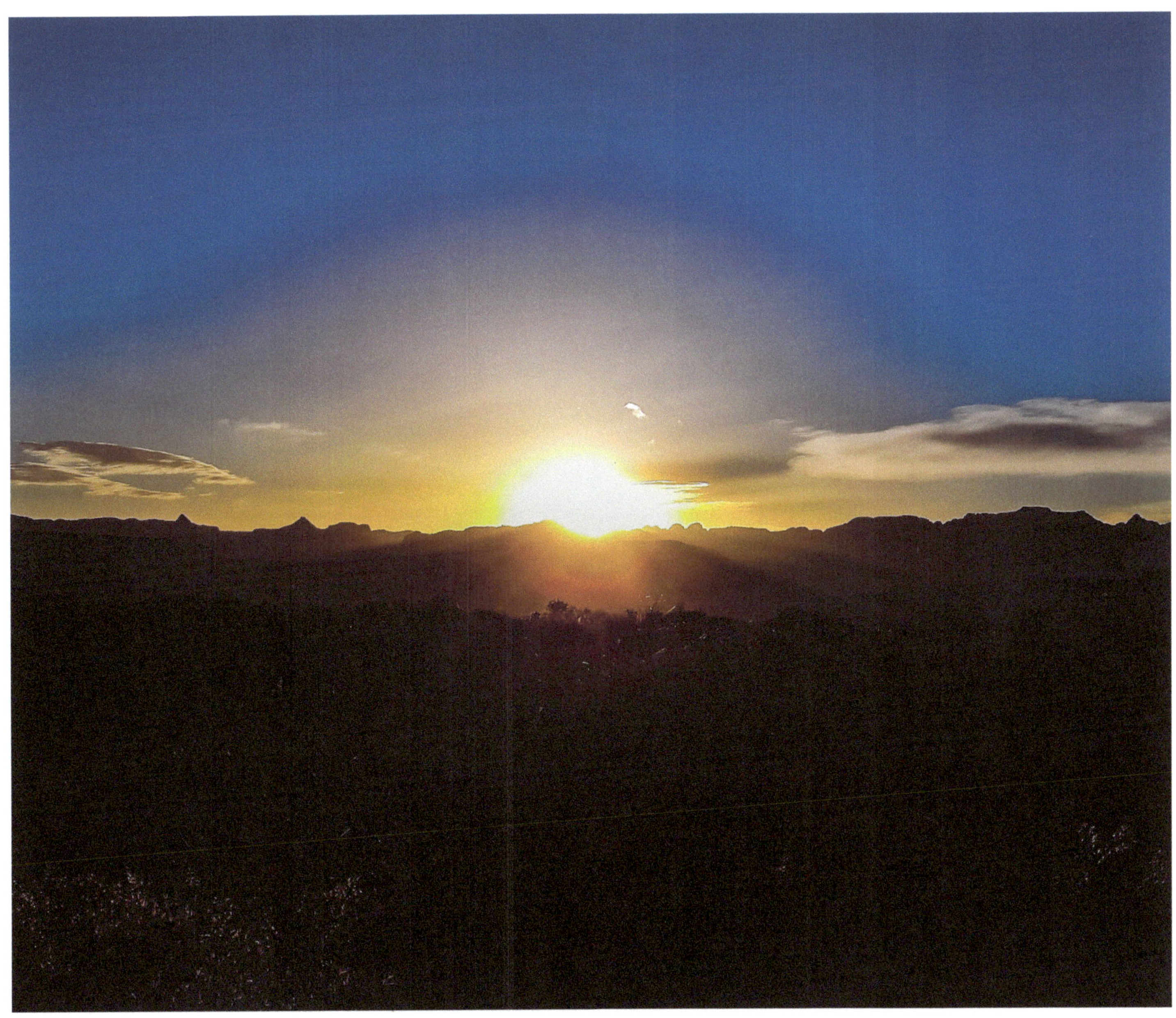

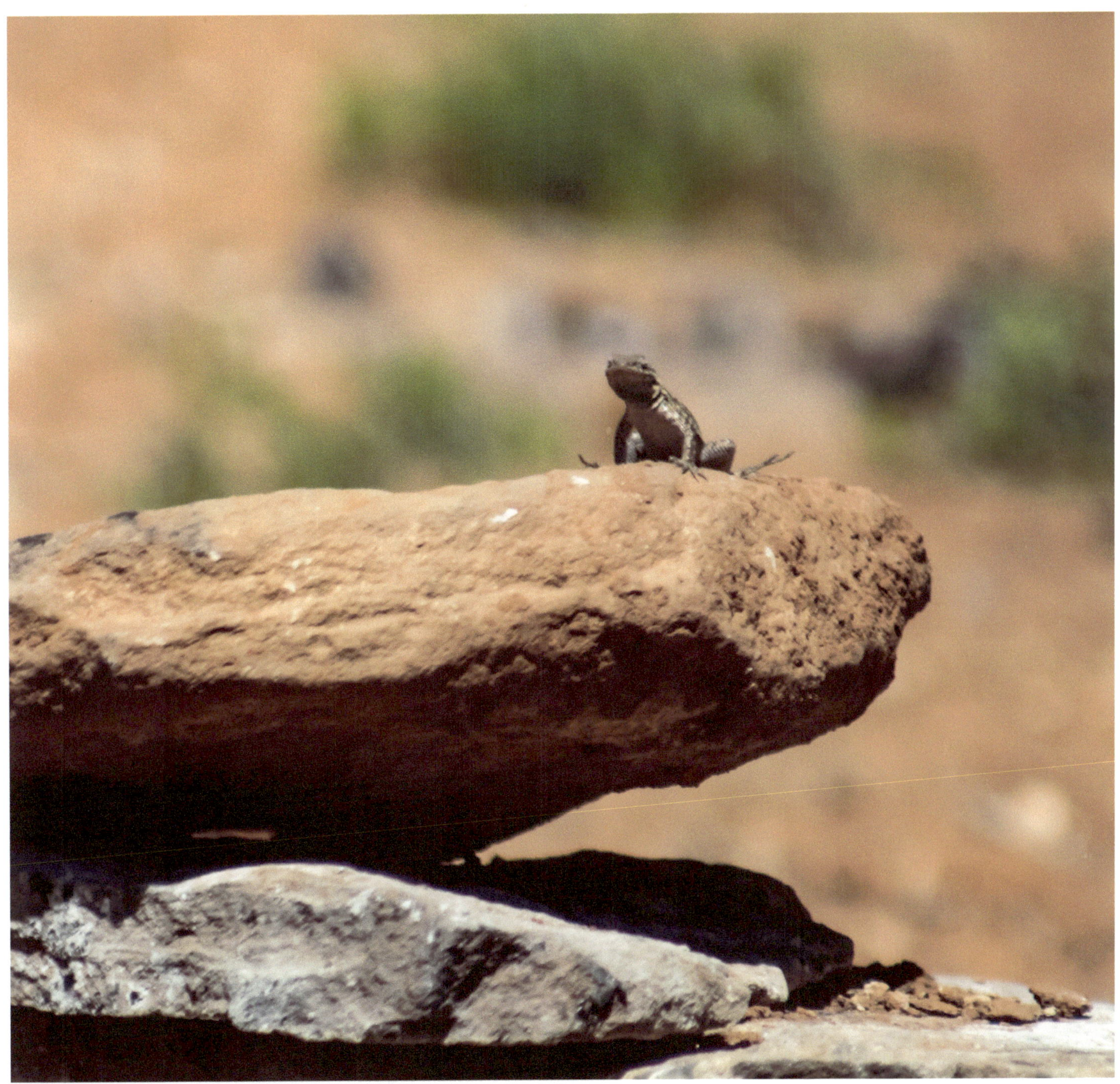

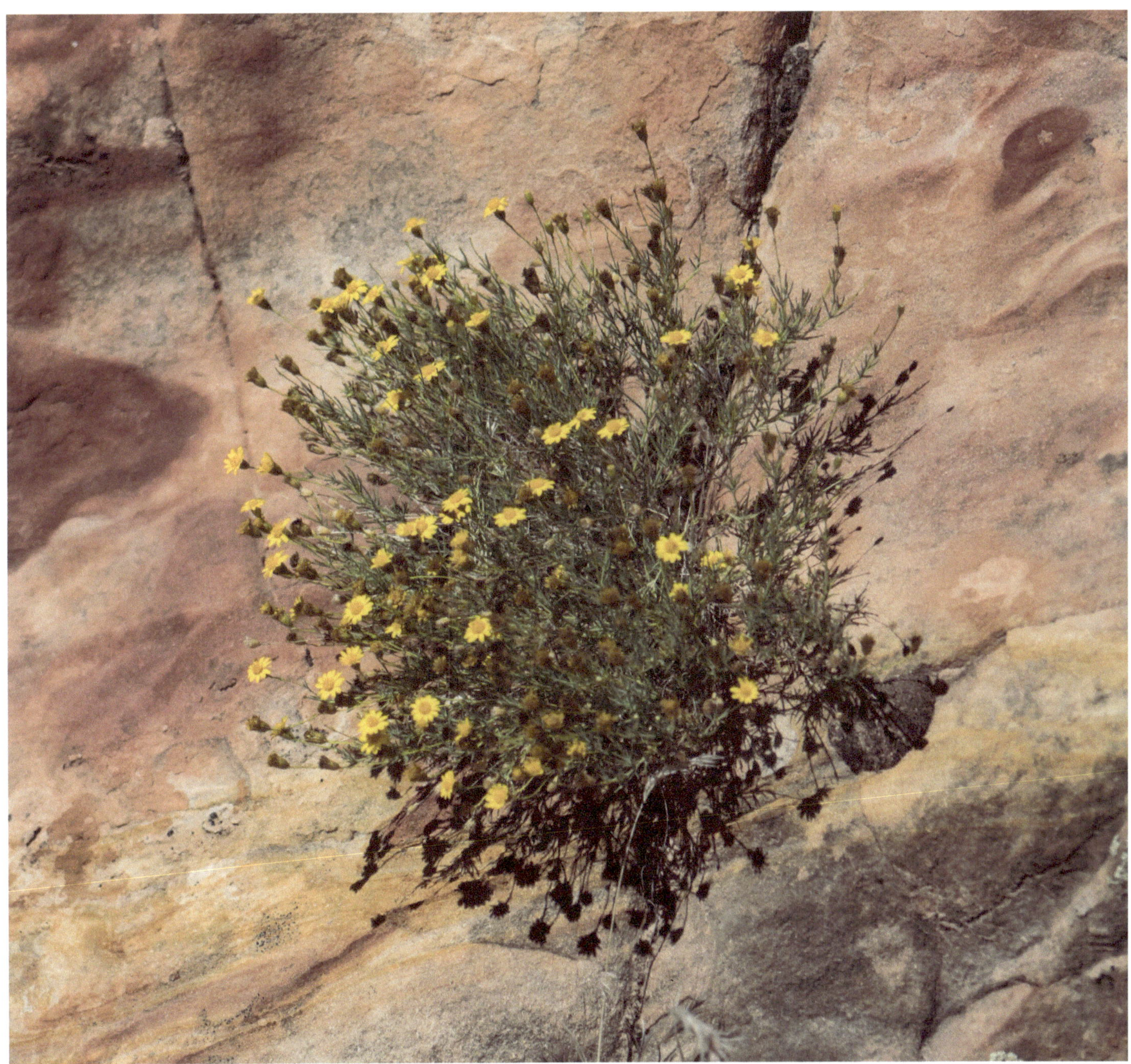

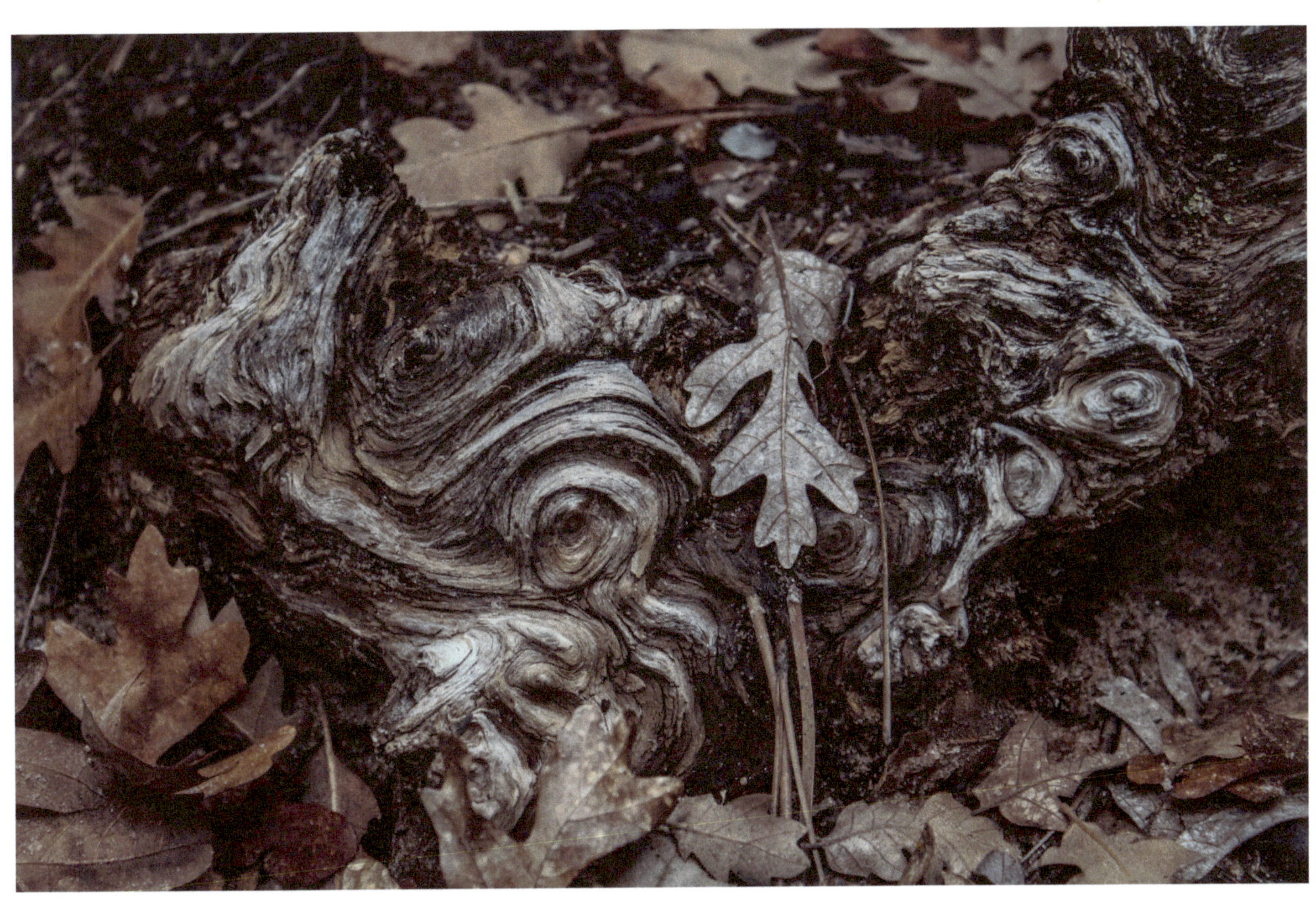

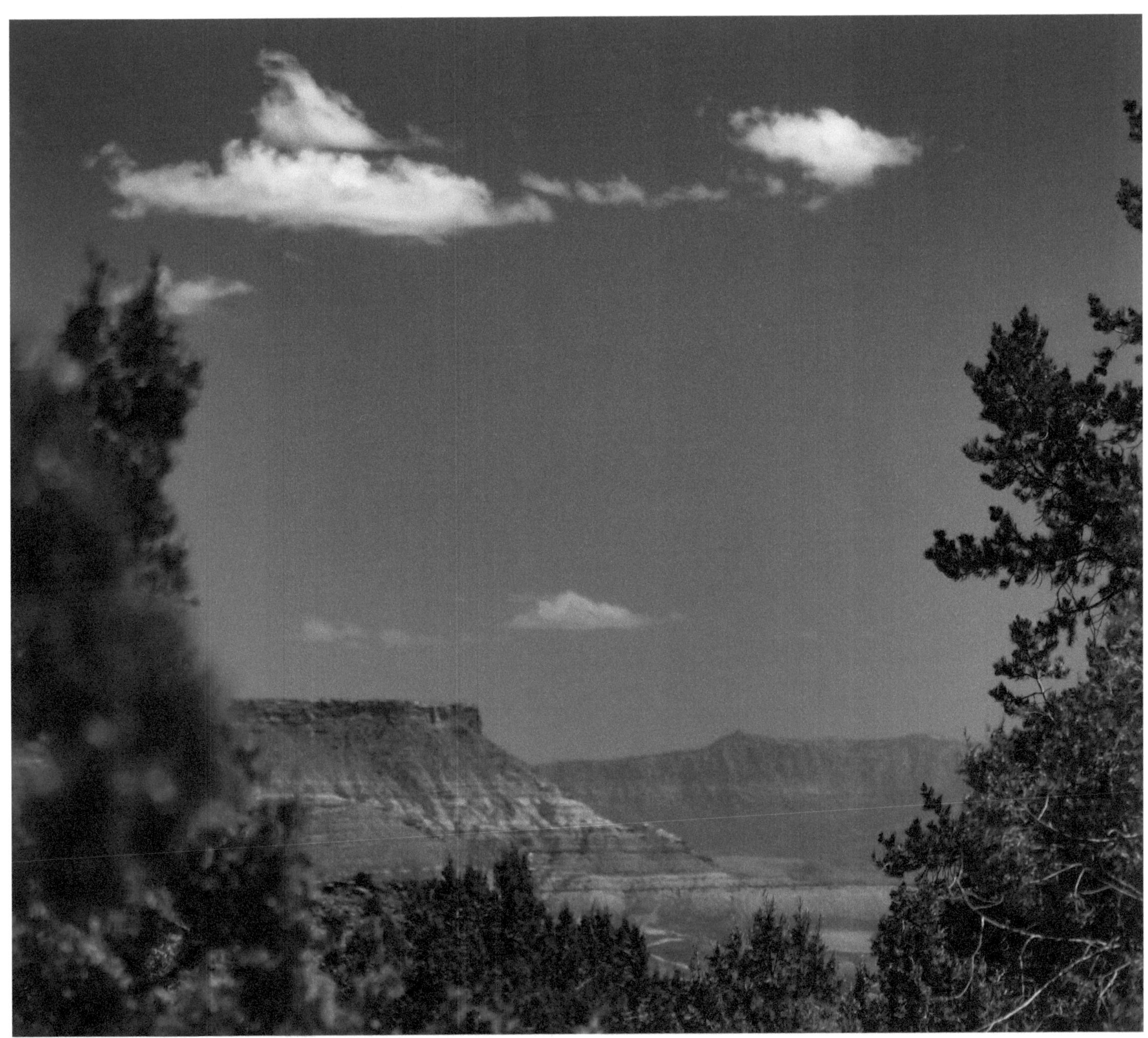

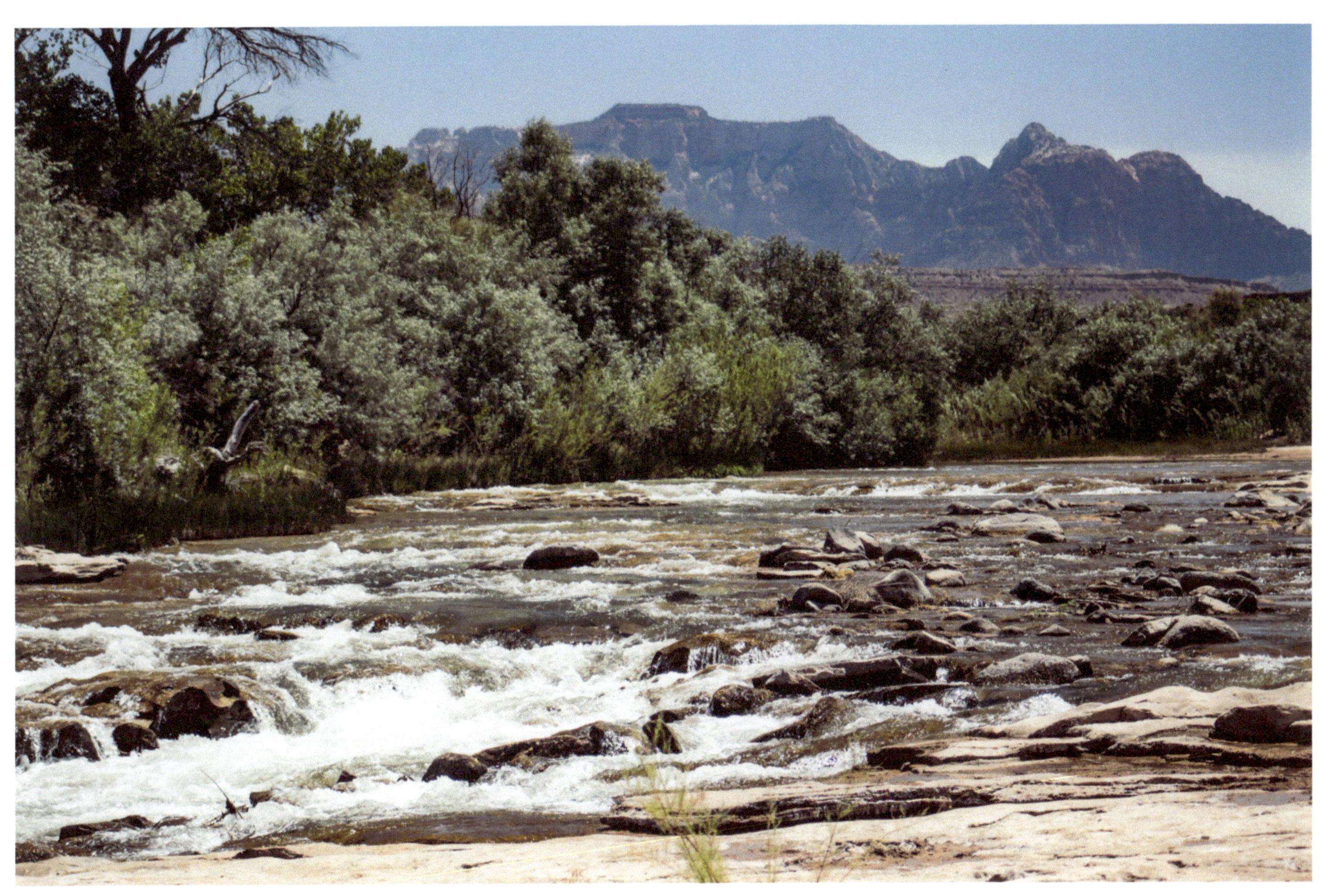

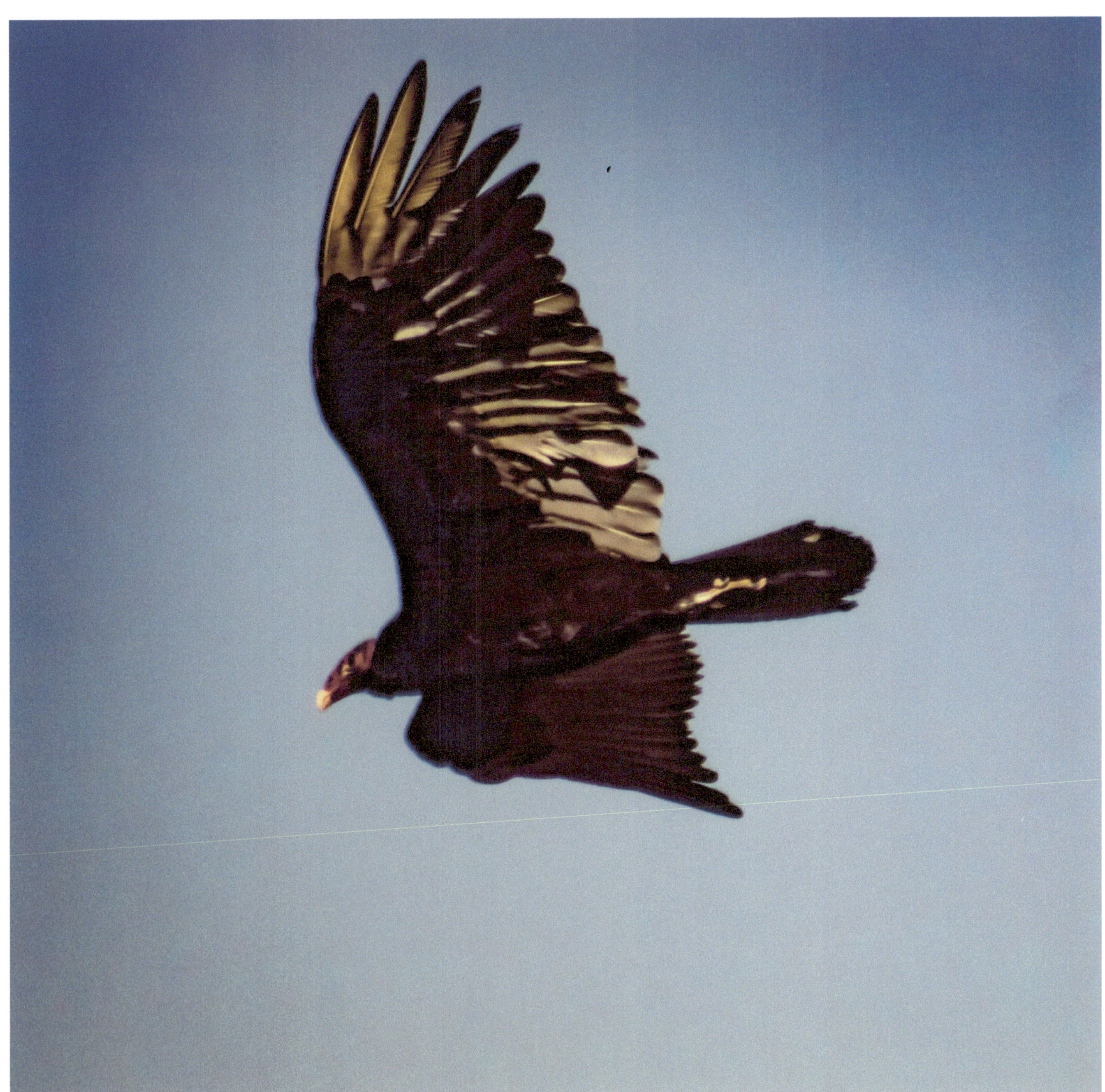

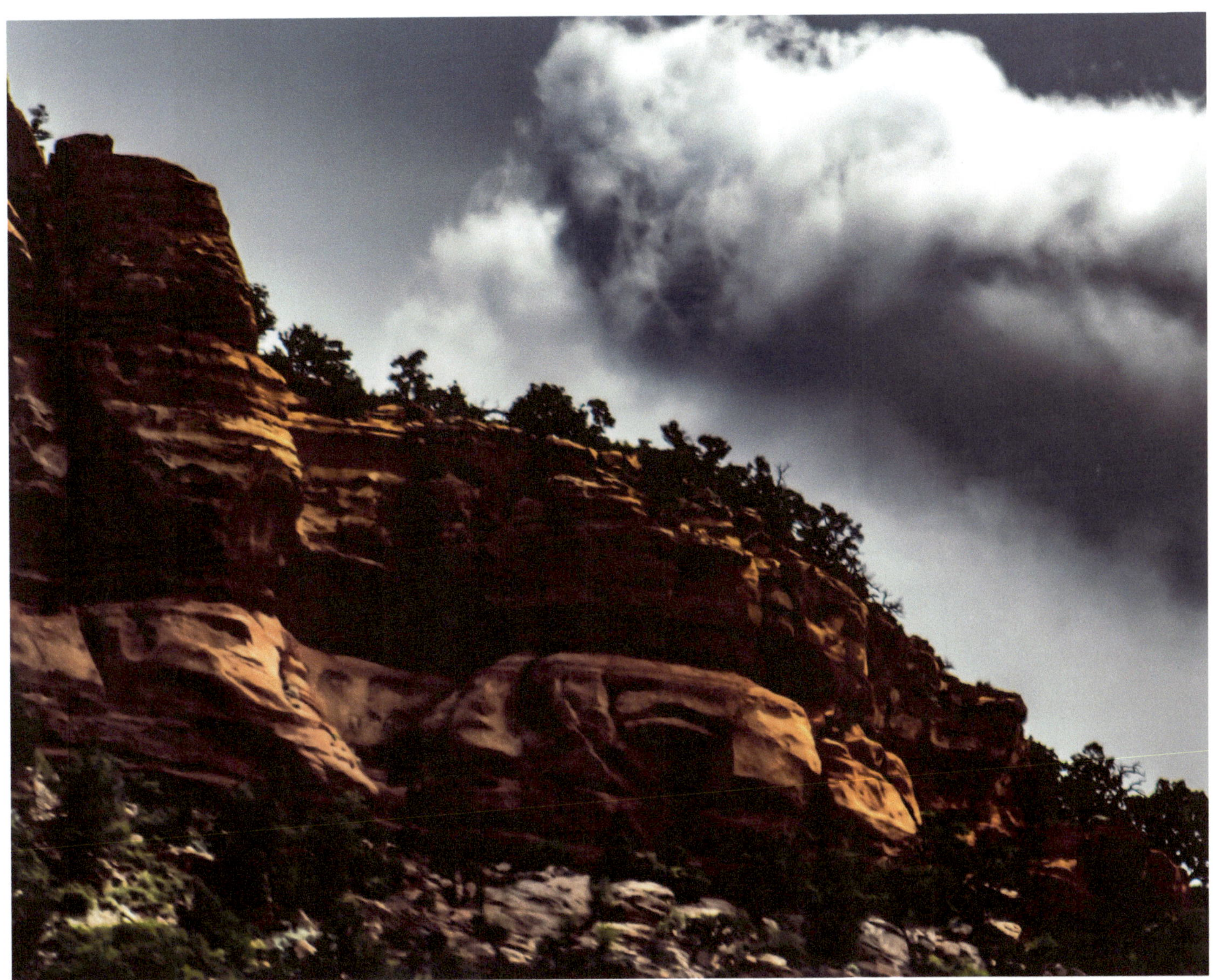

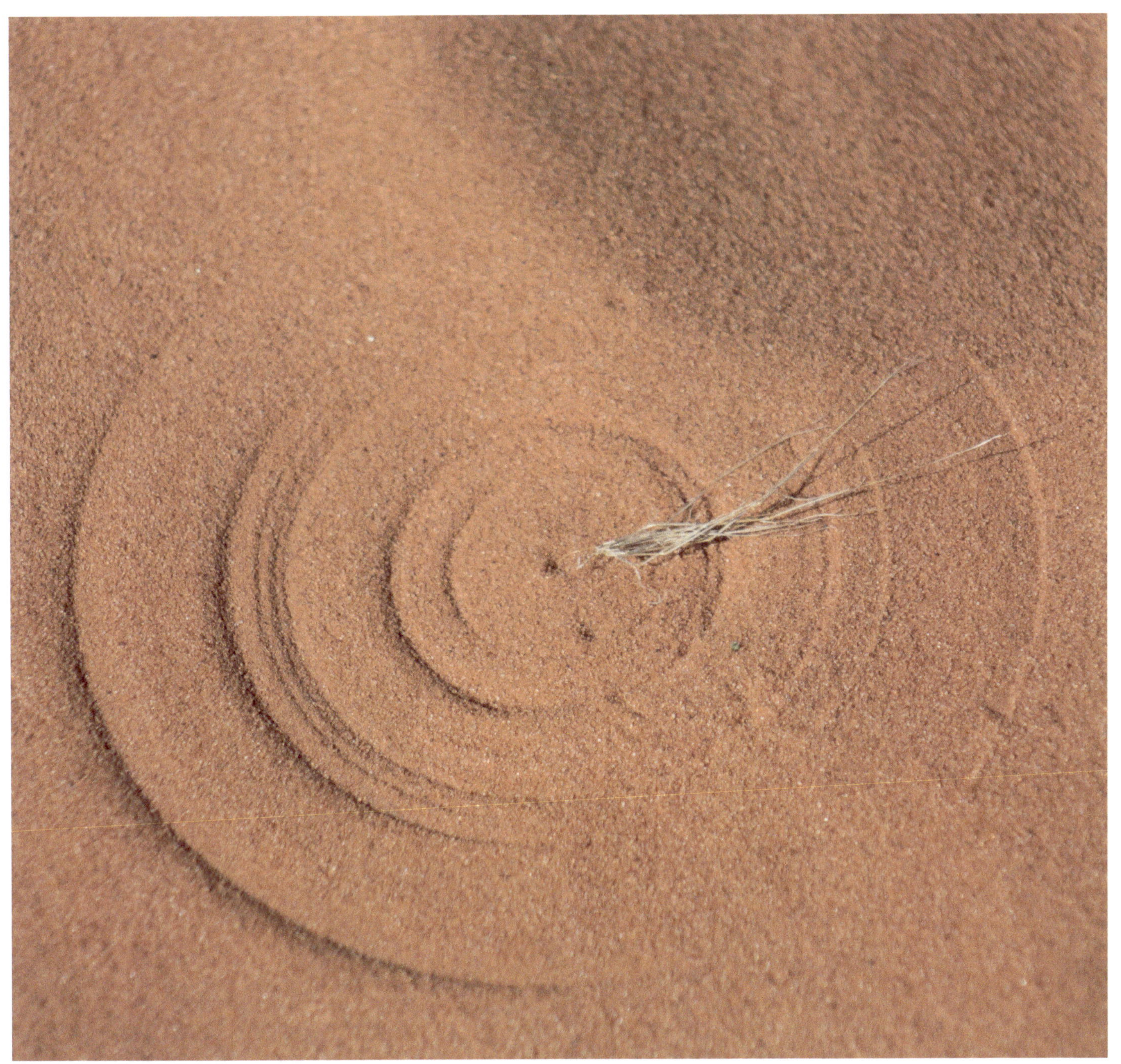

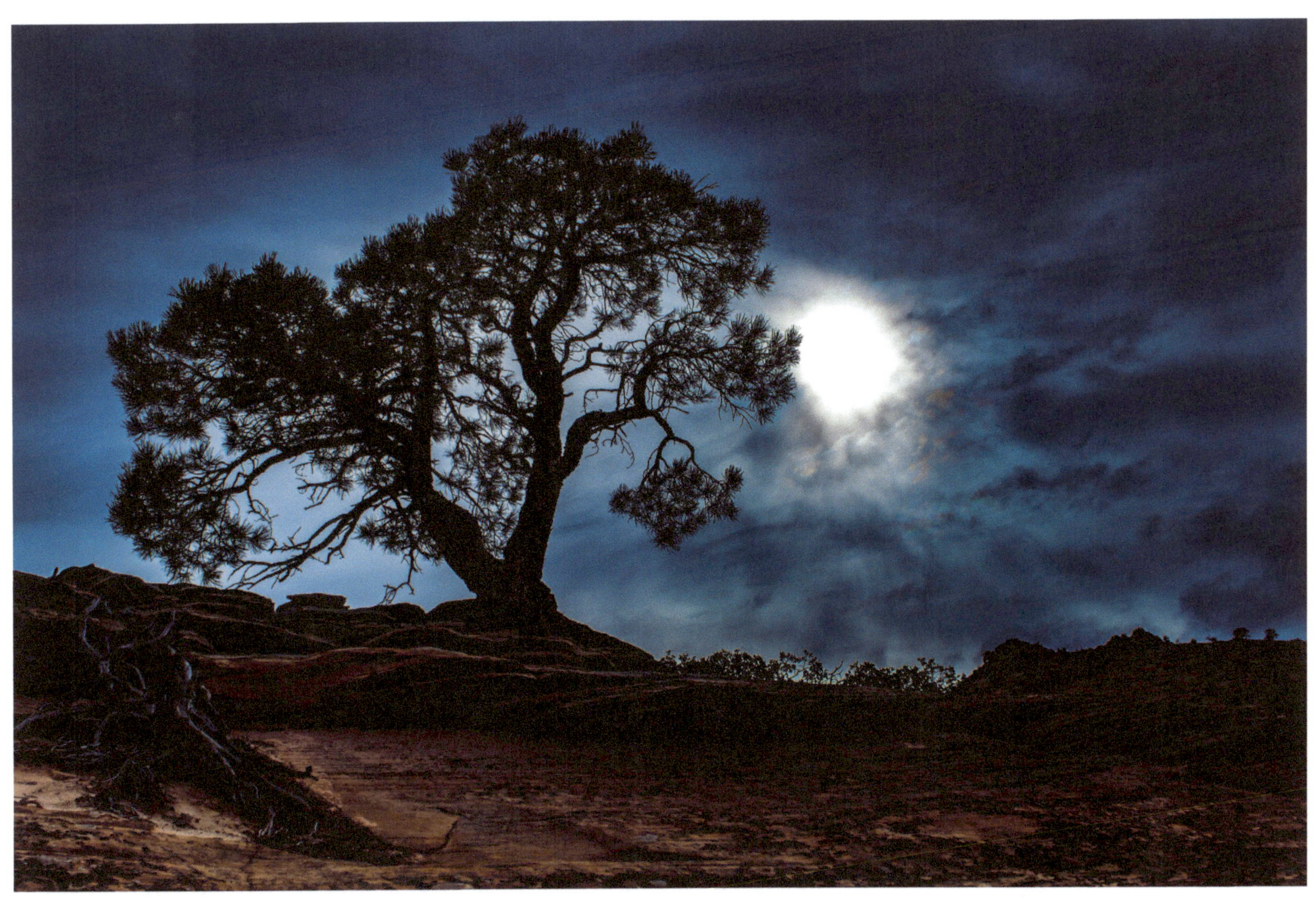

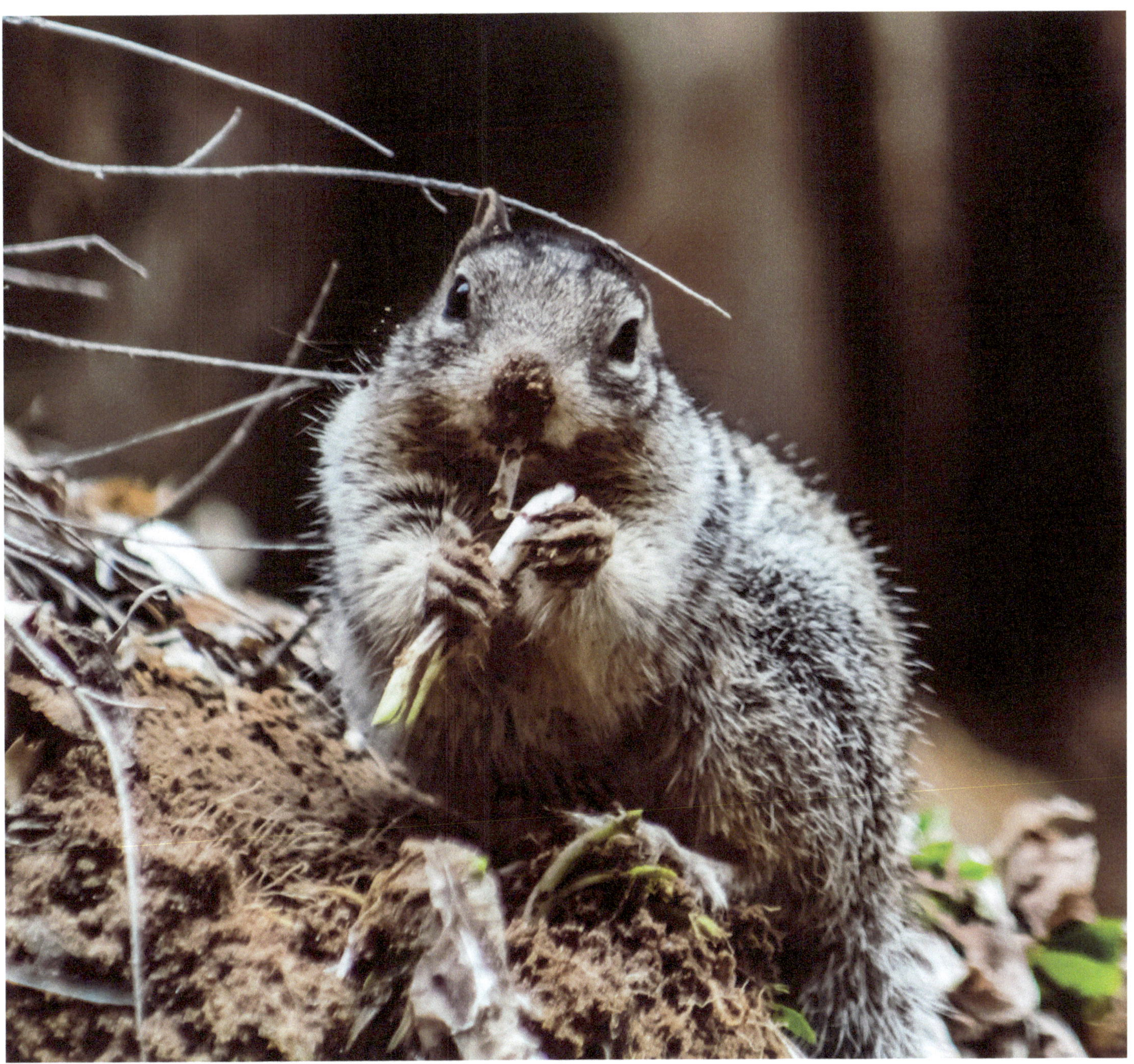

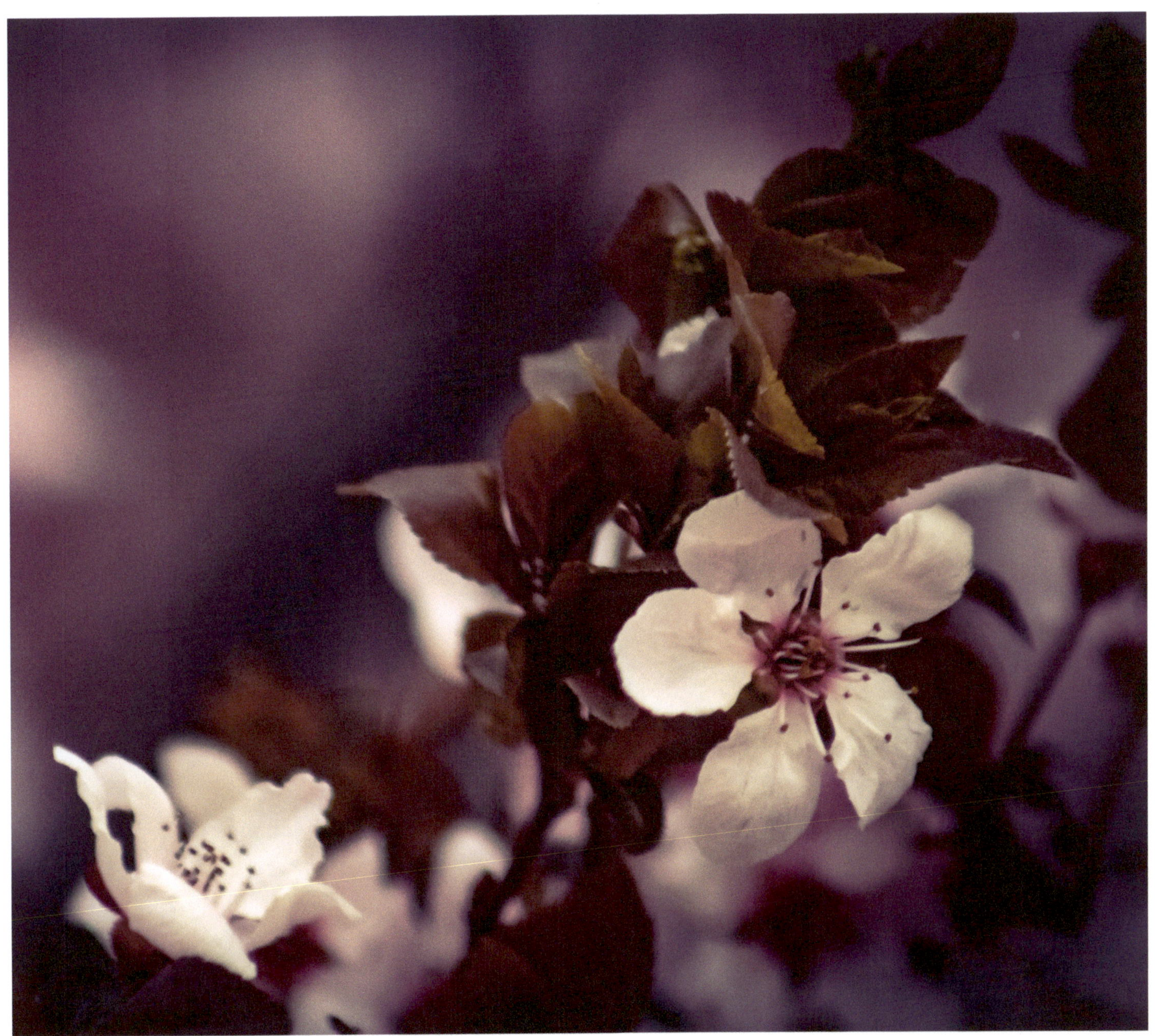

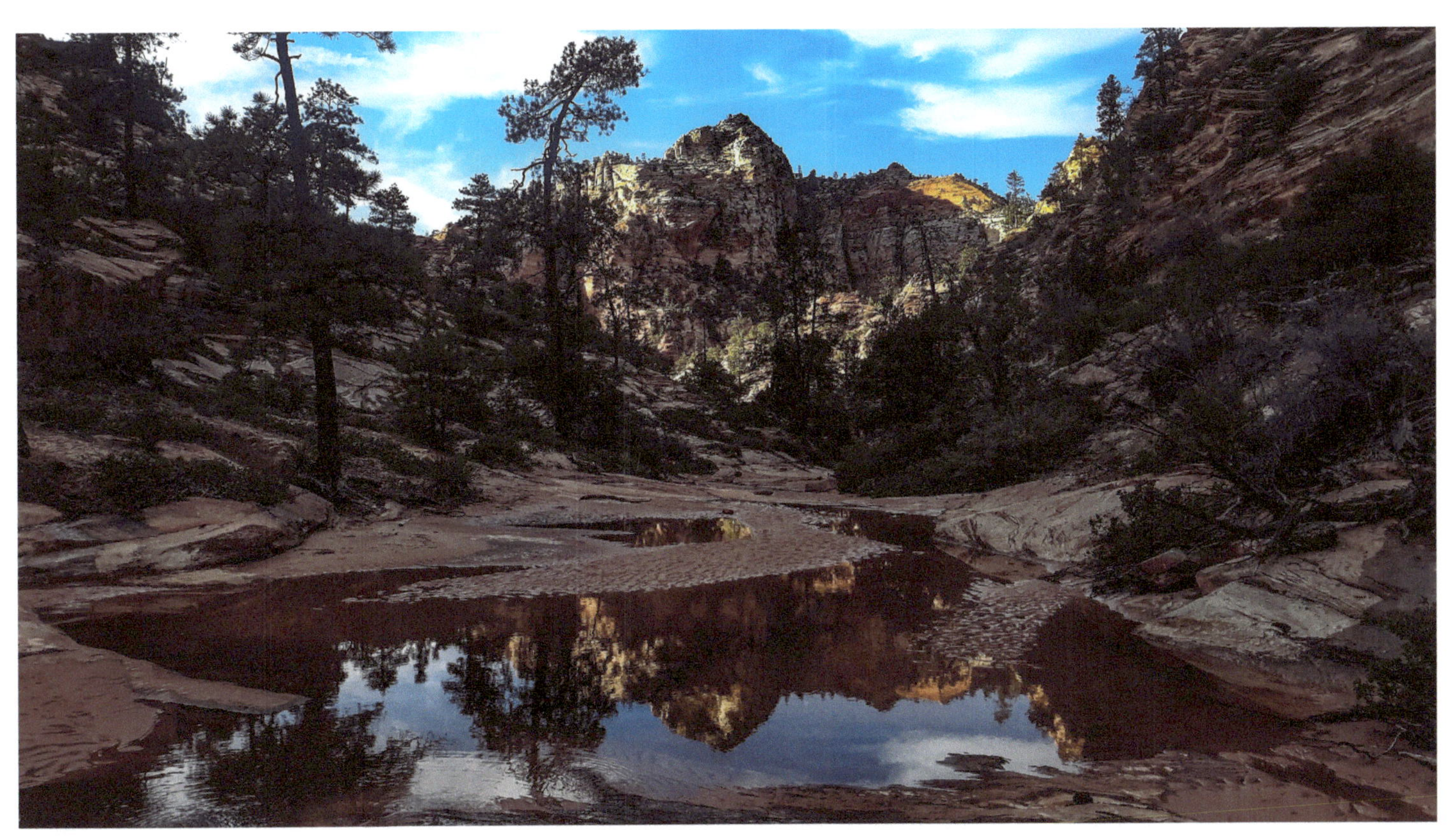

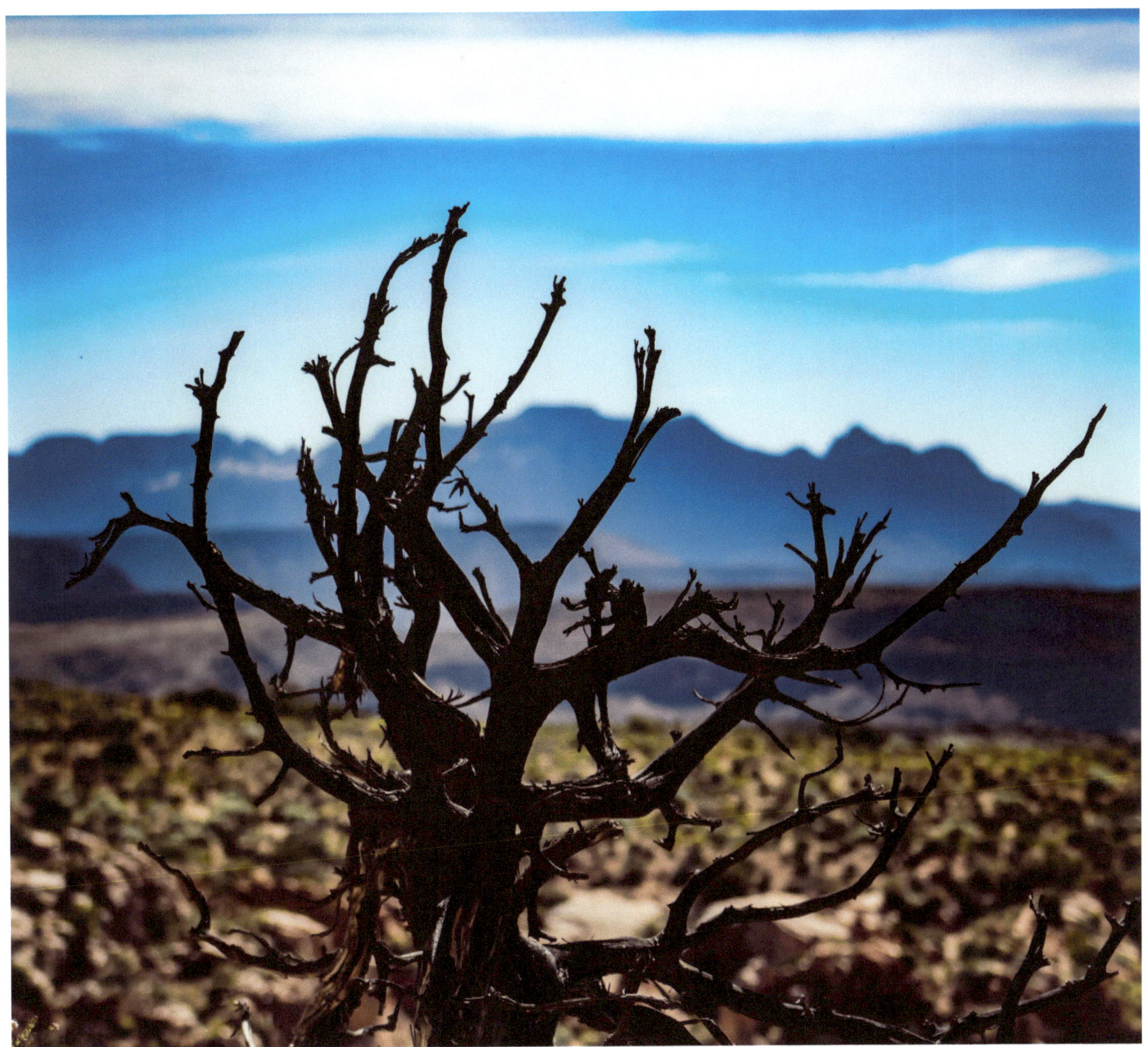

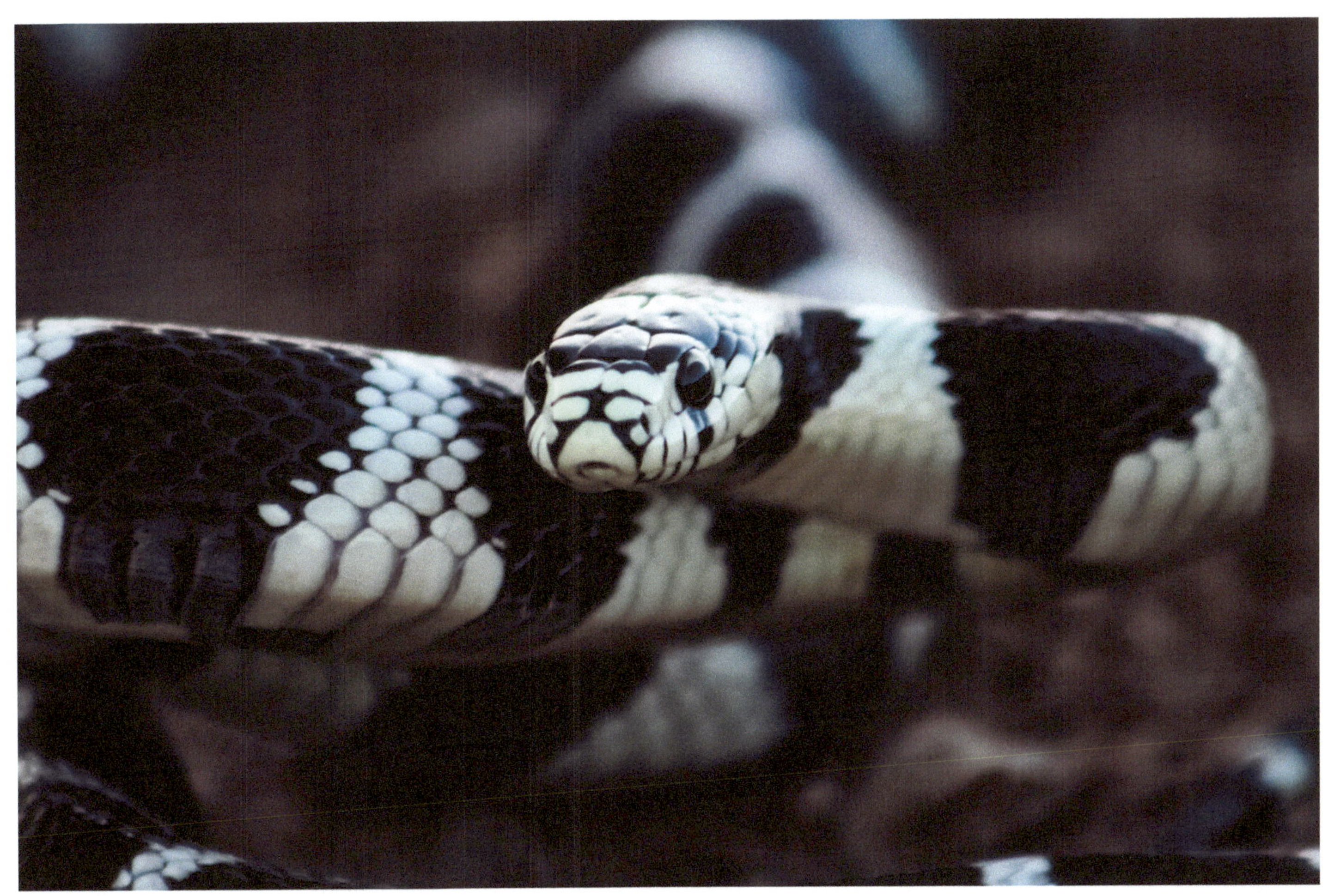

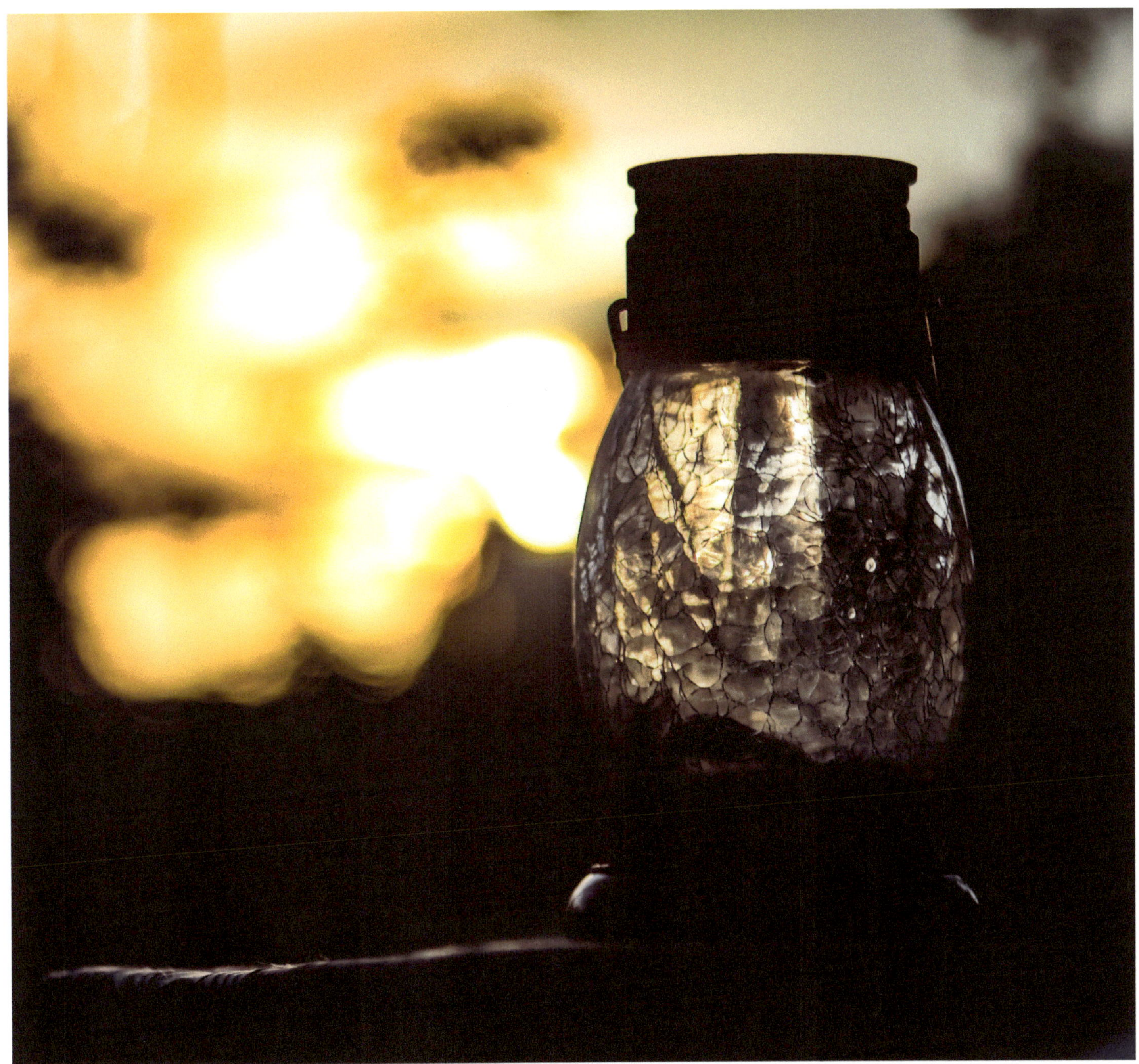

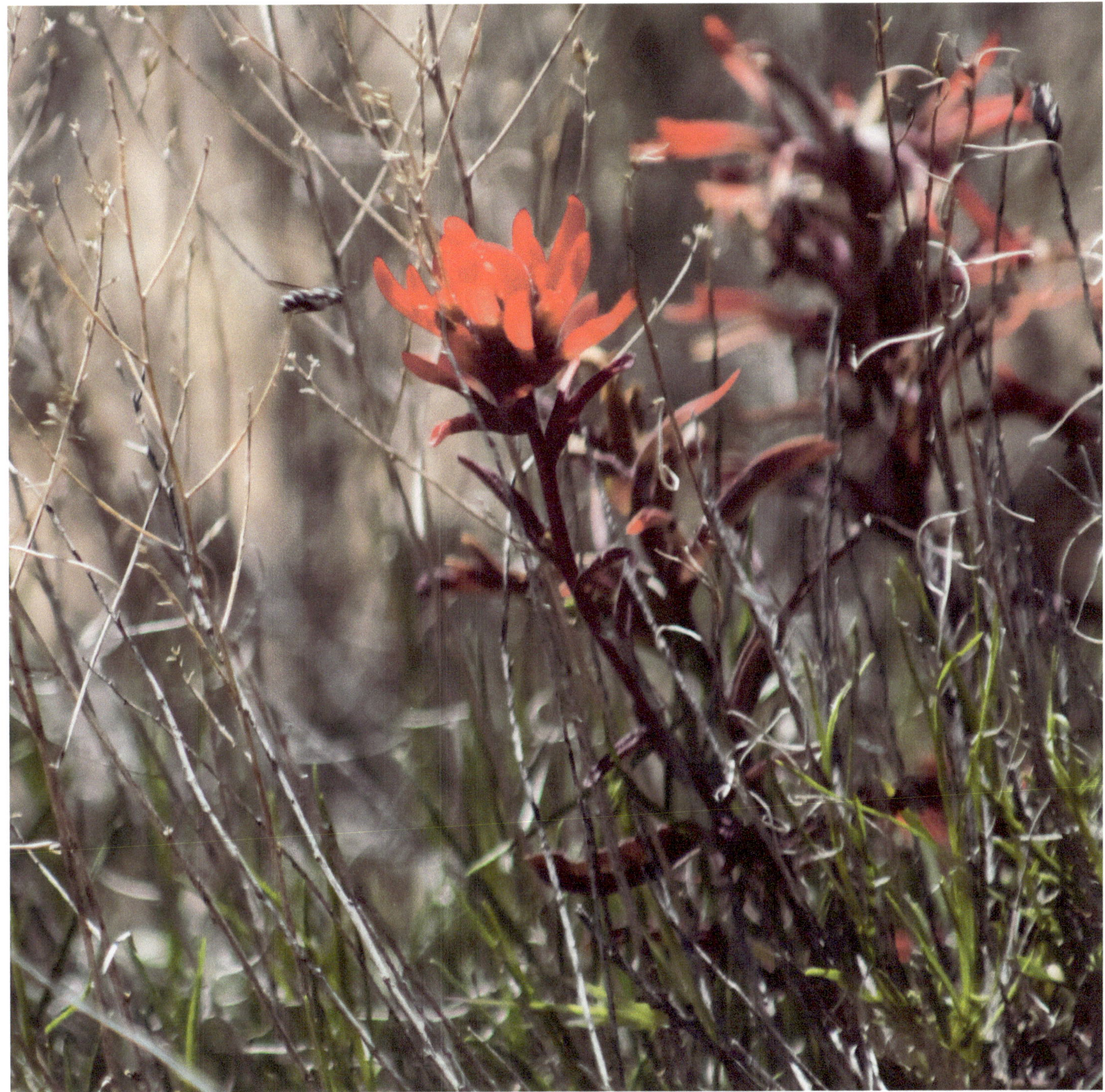

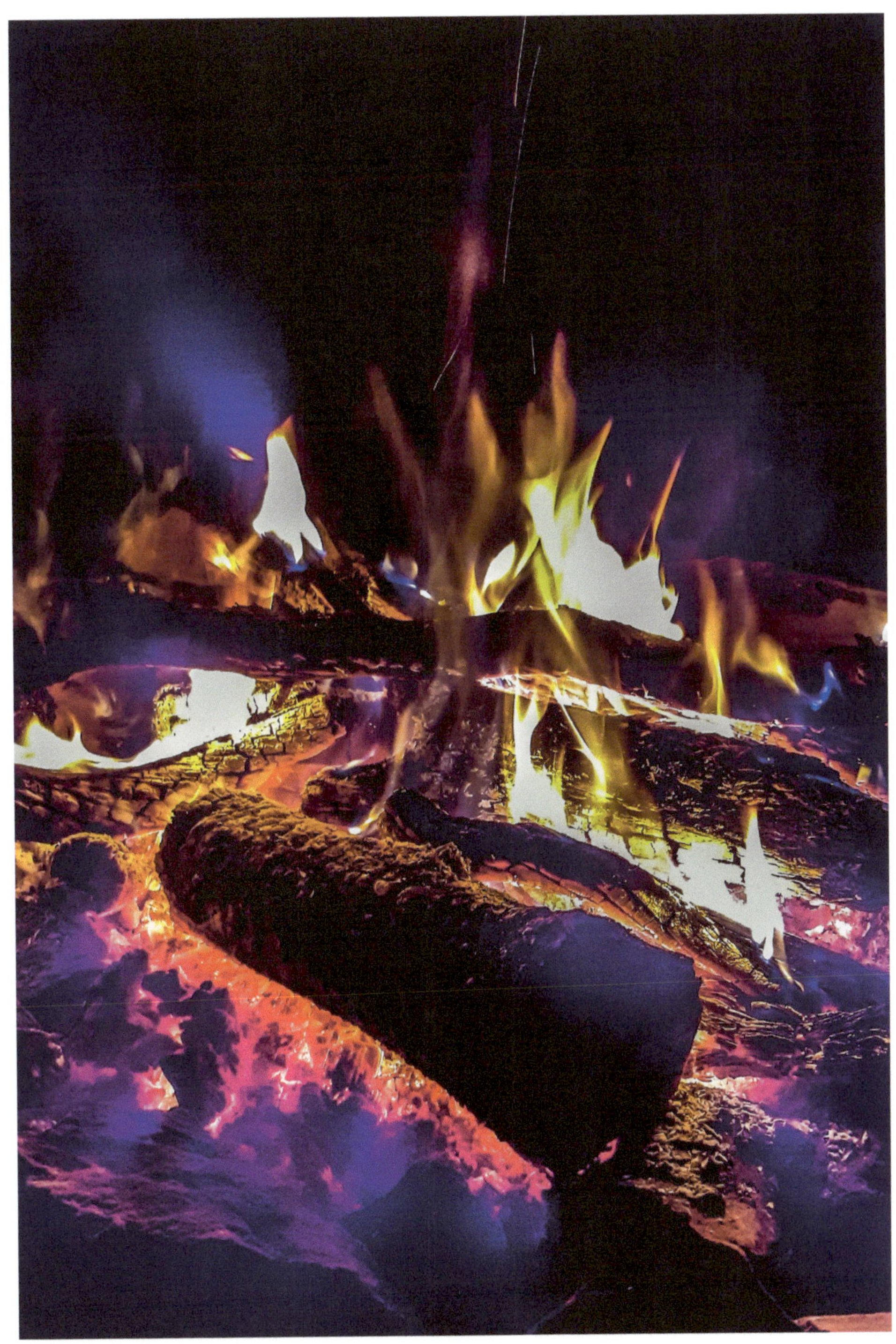

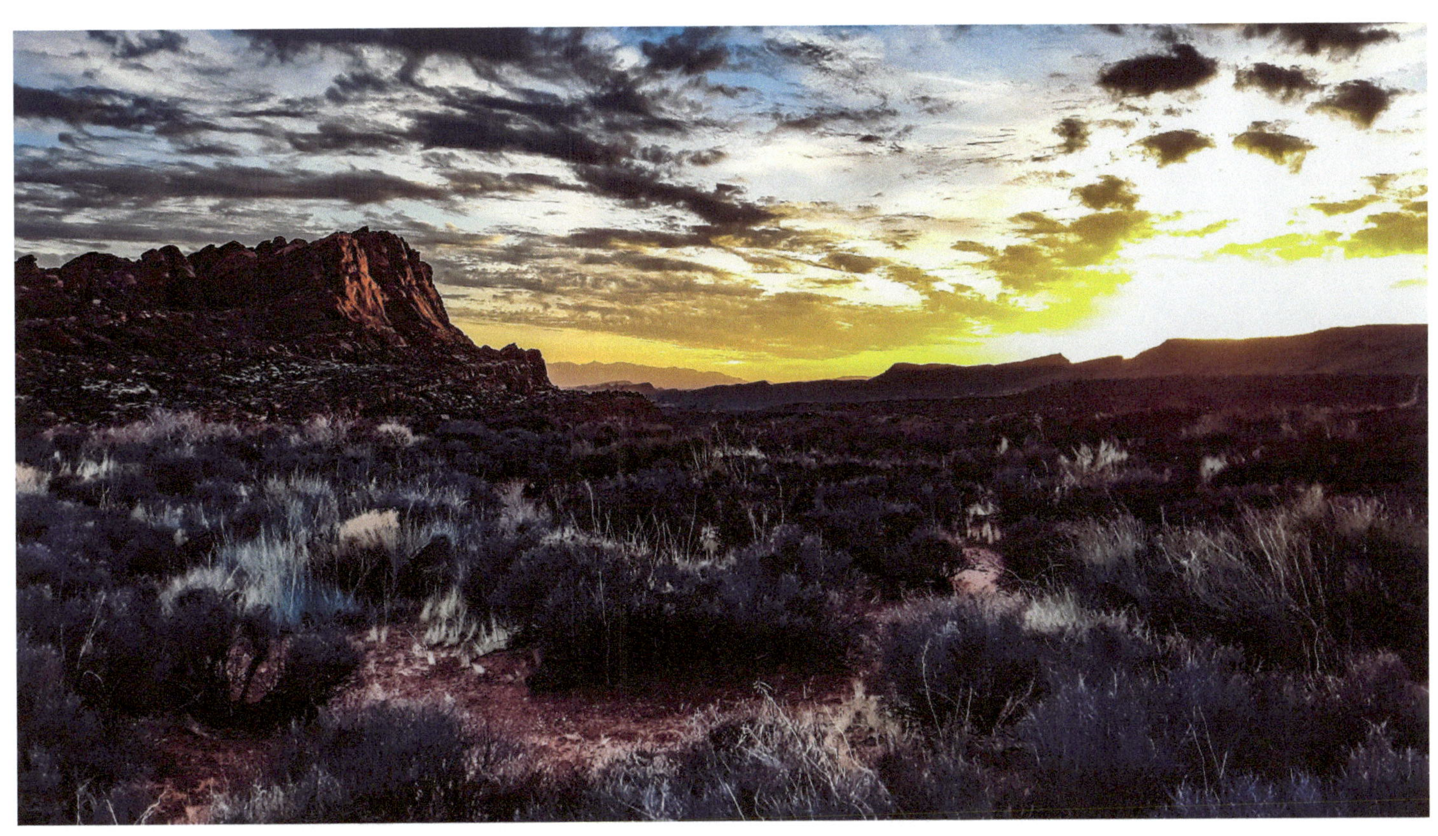

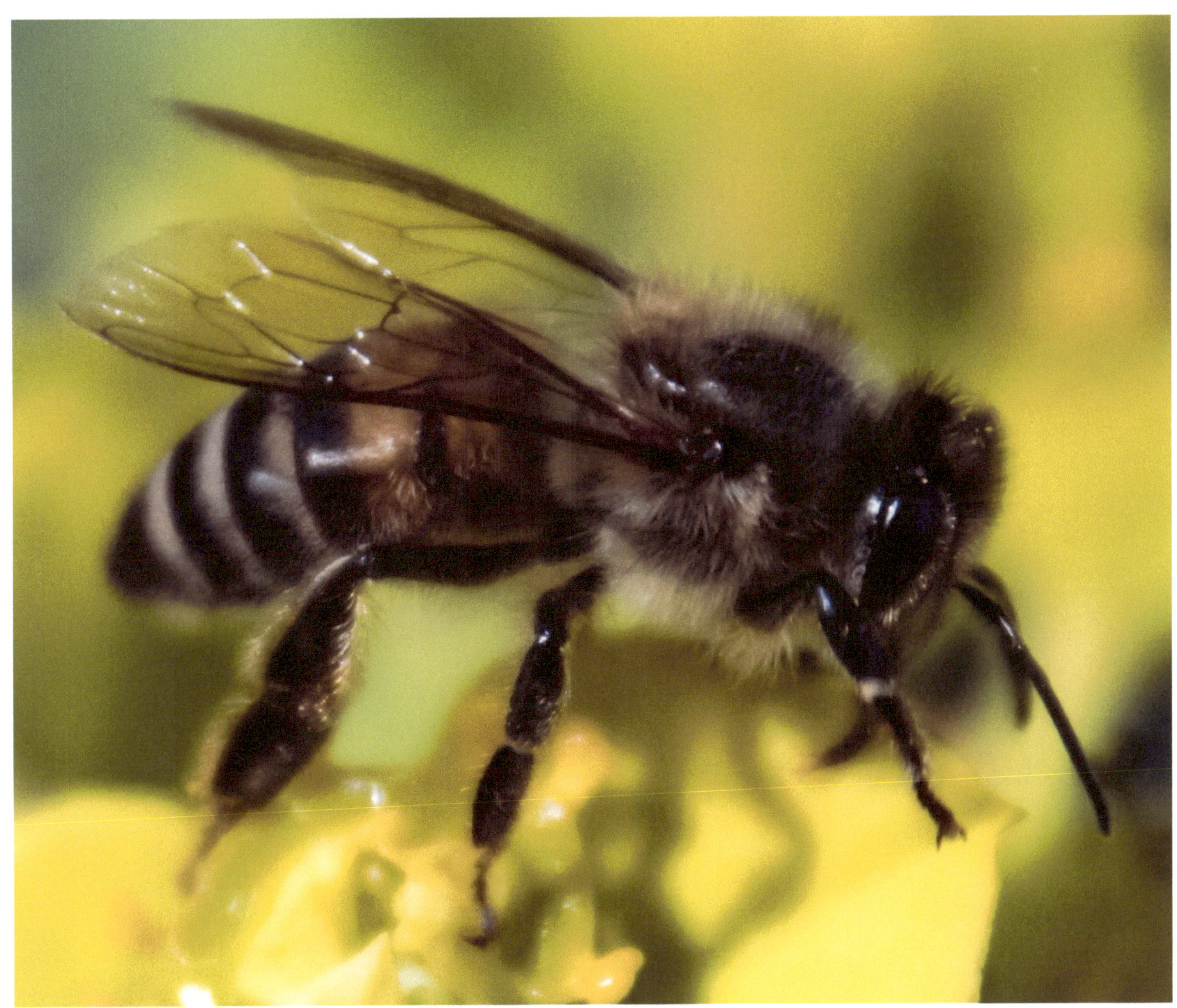

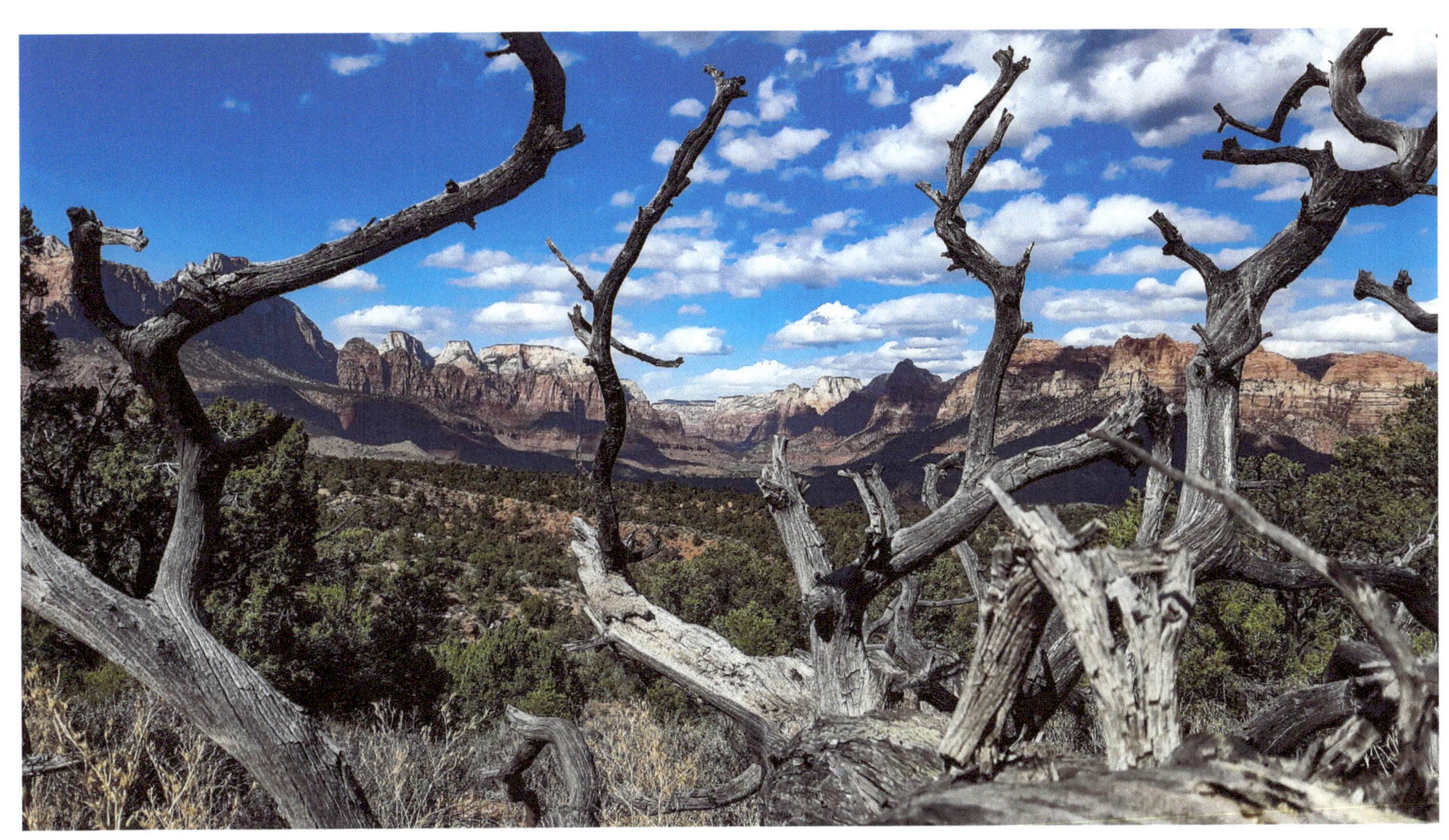

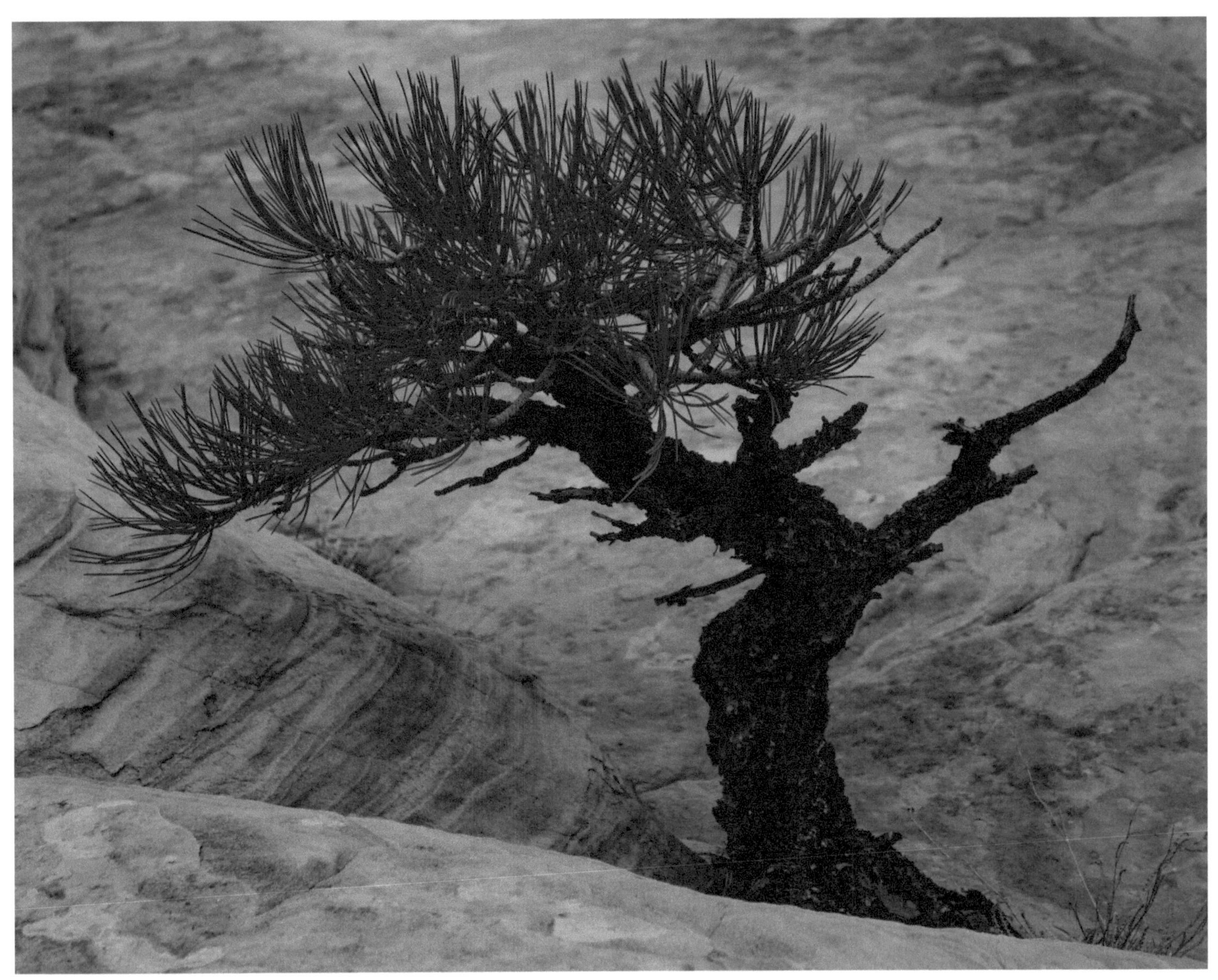

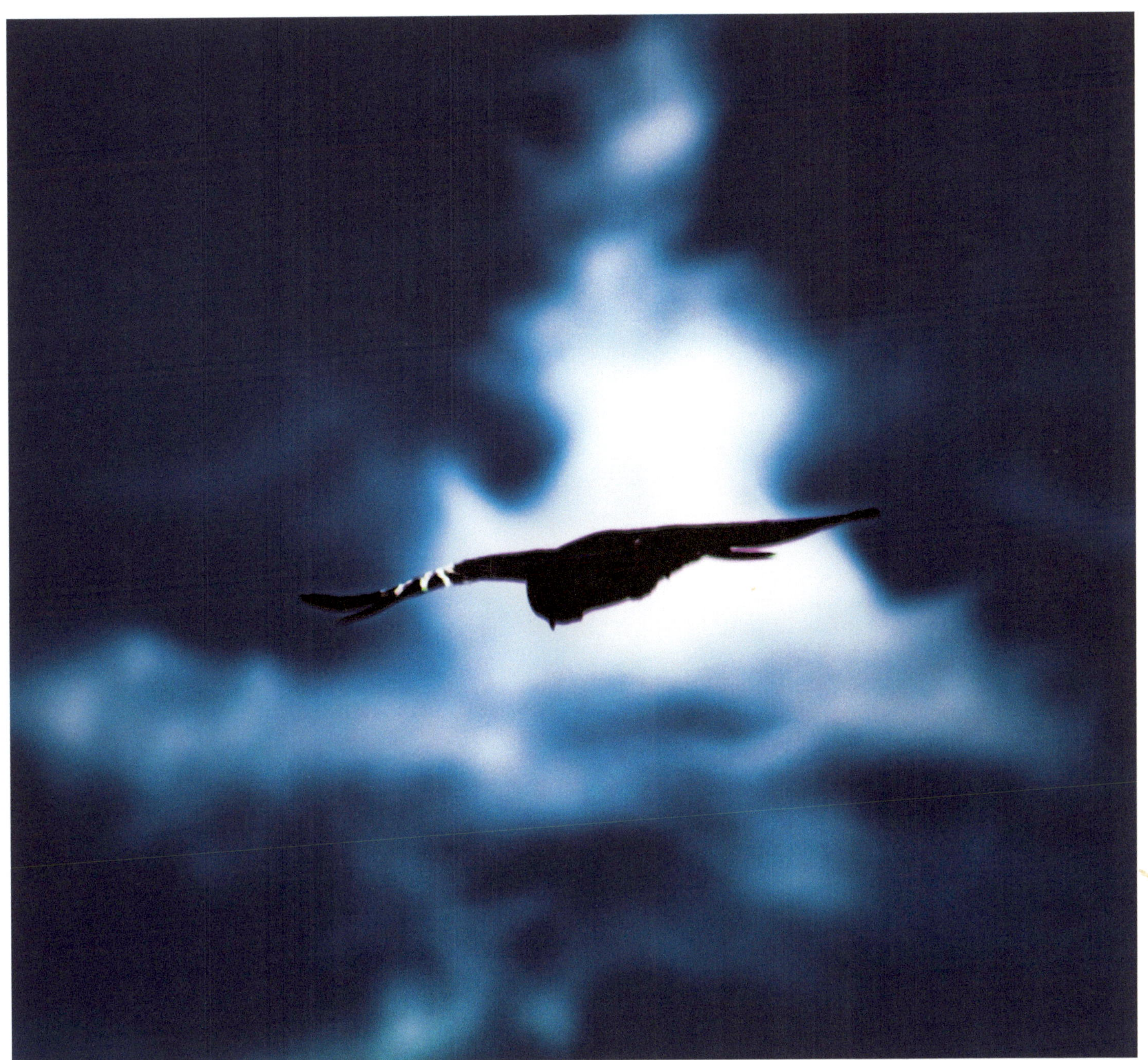

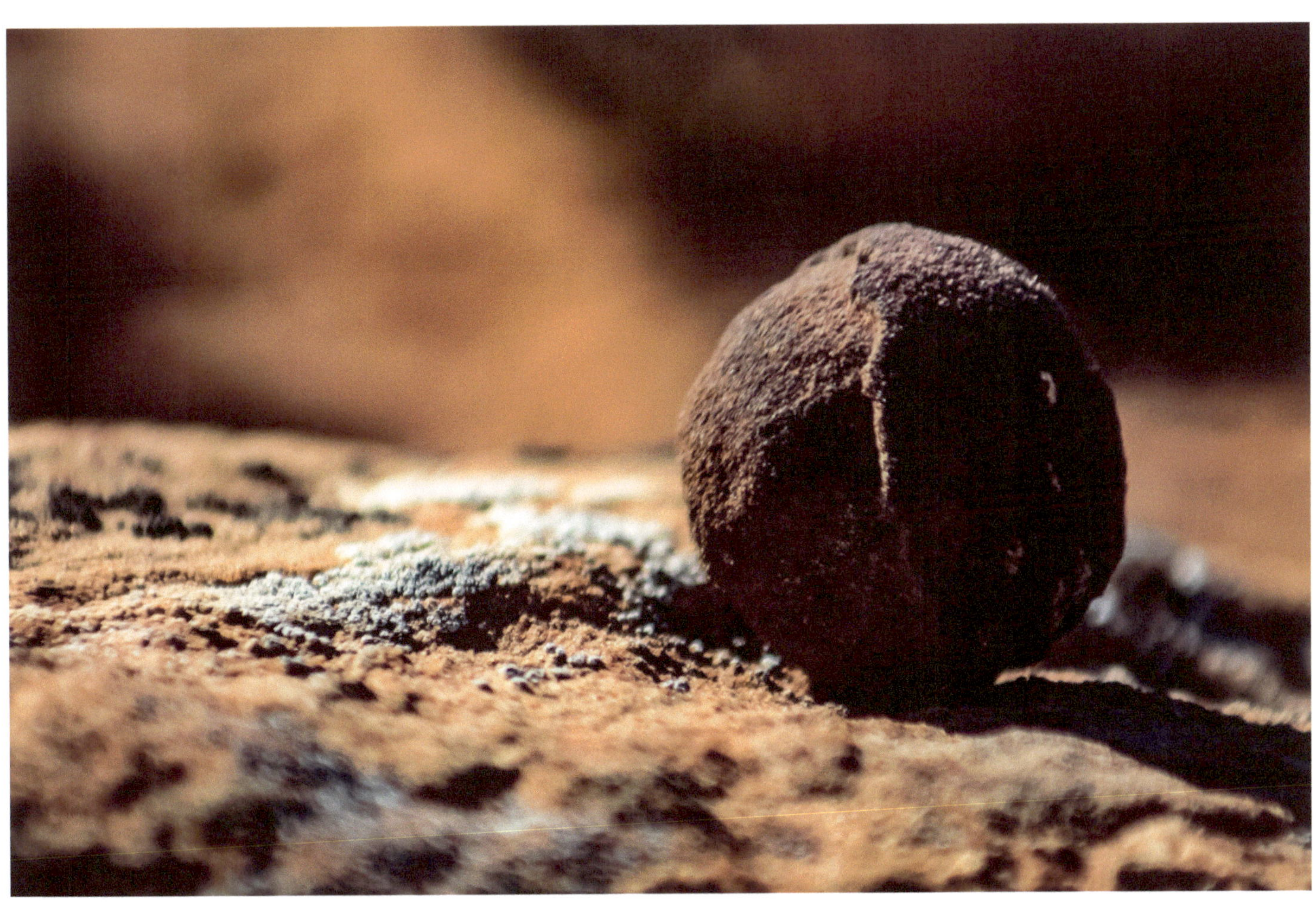

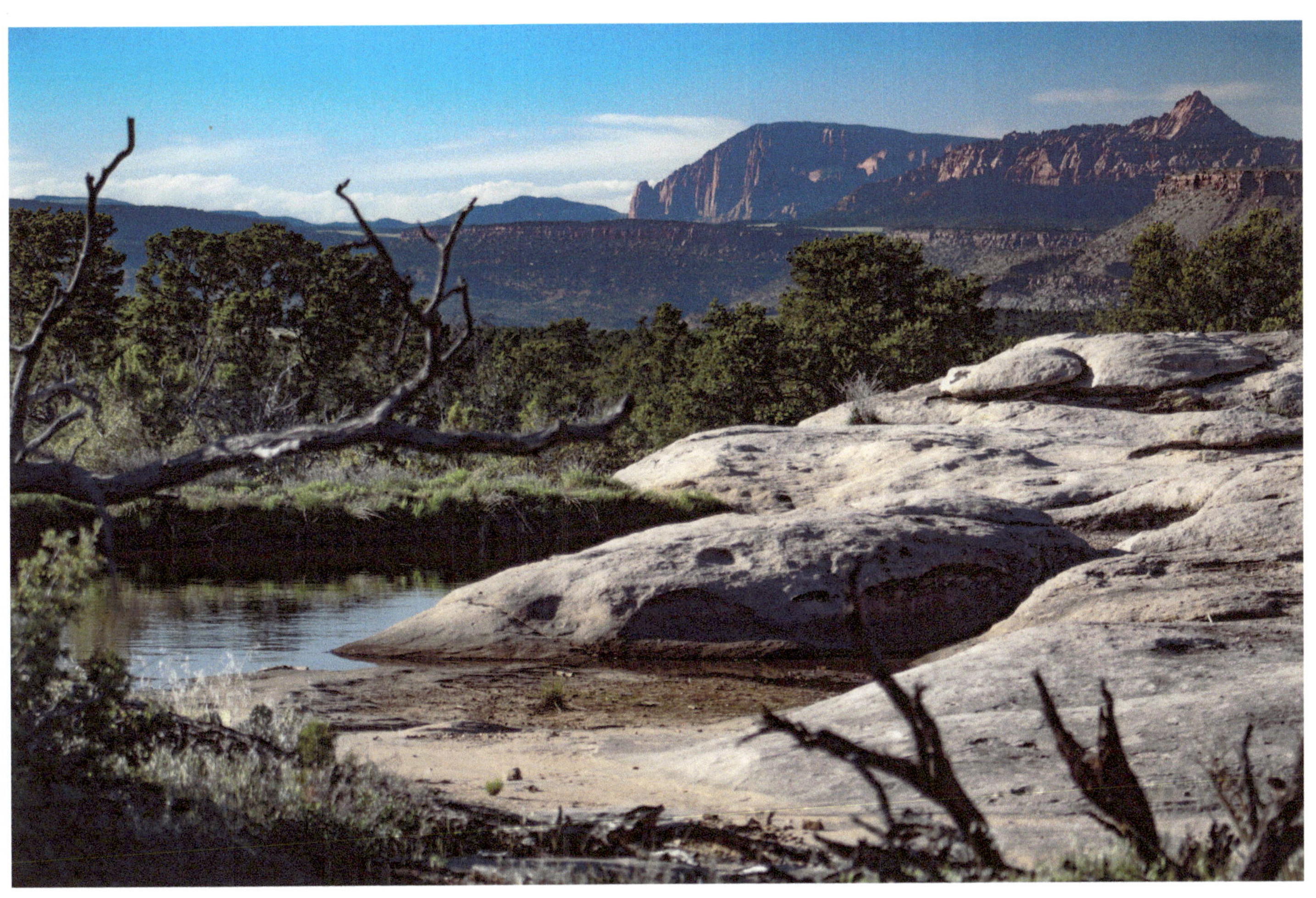

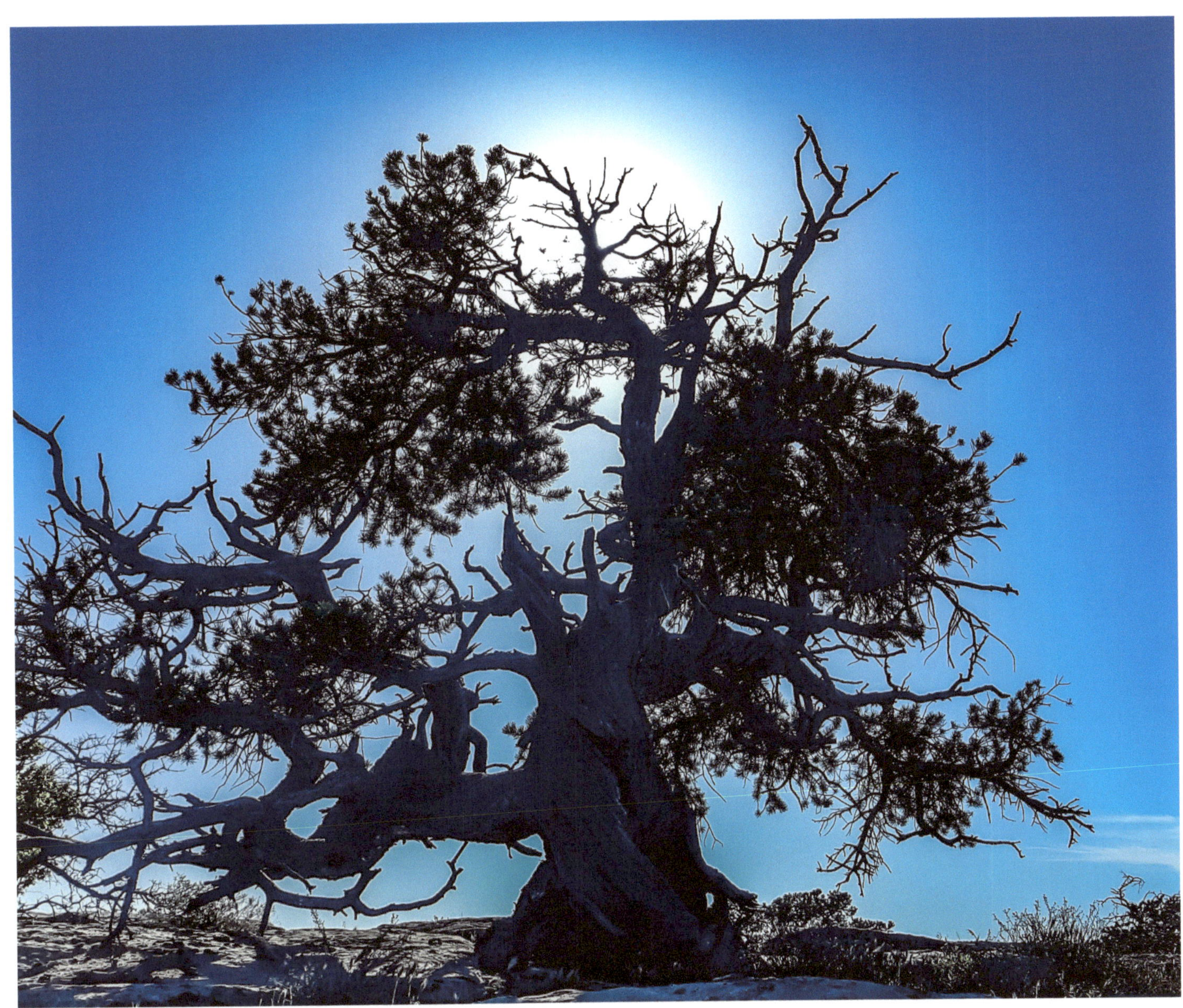

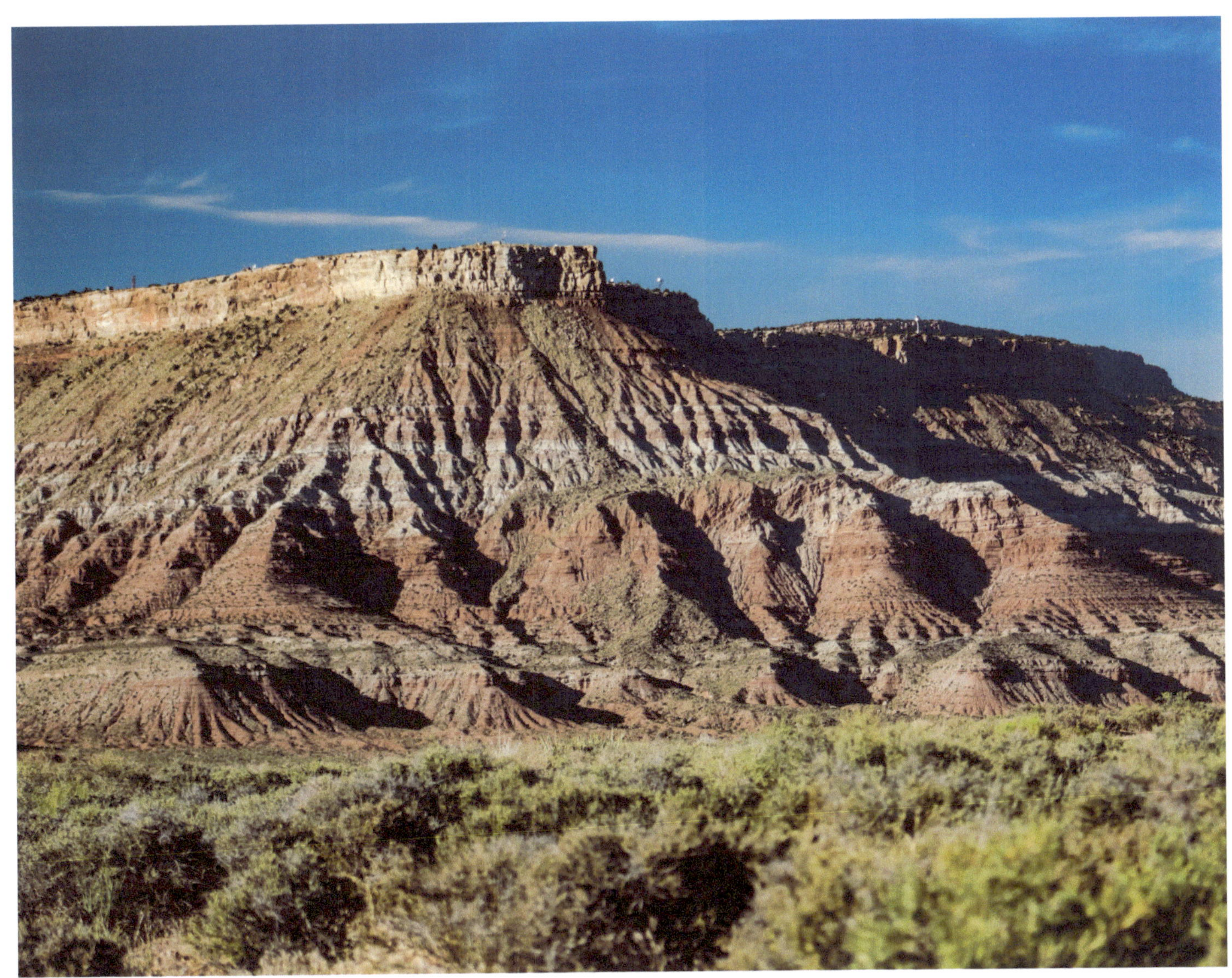

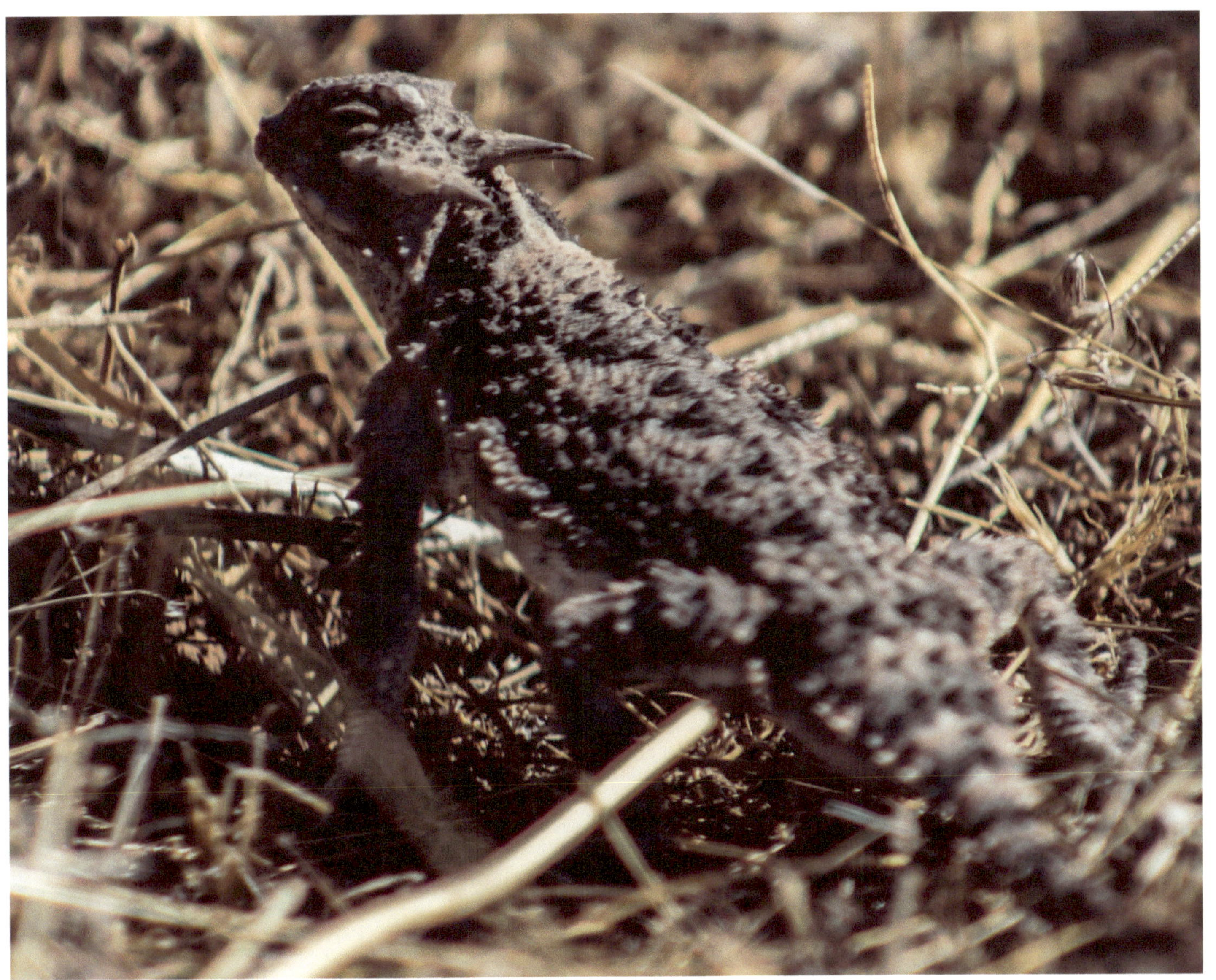

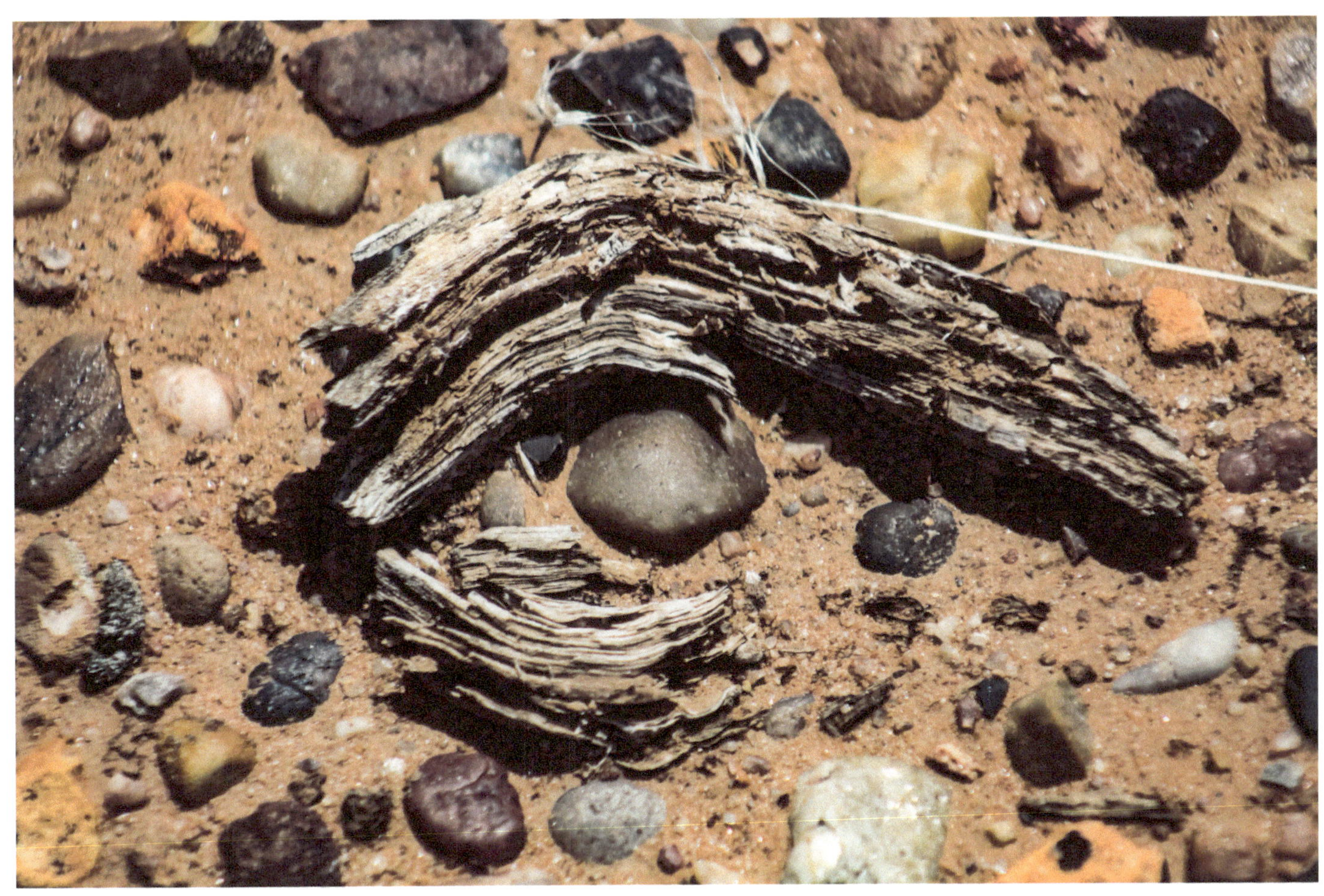

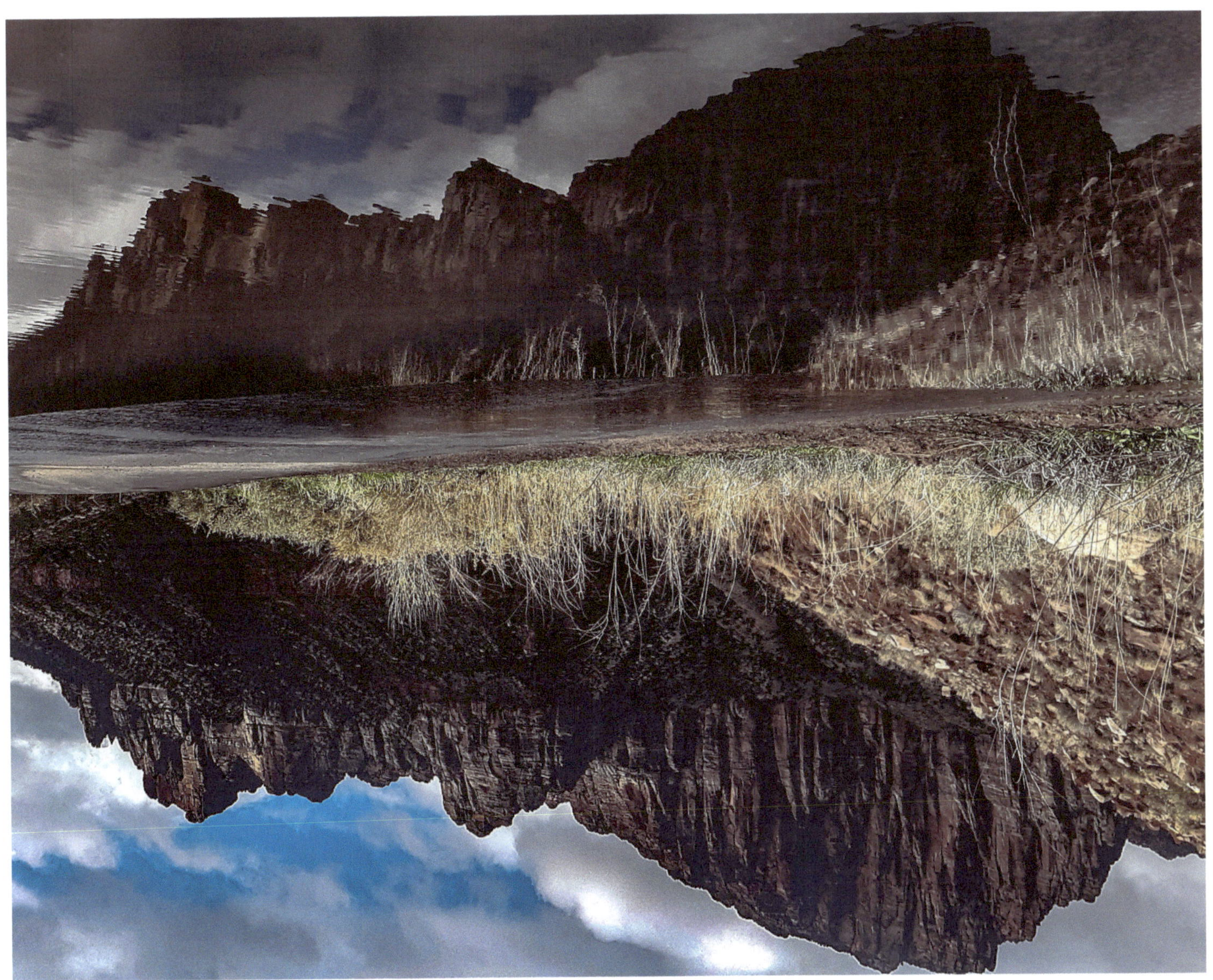

About the Author

Joshua Pettit is a photographer living and working in Southern Utah. His photography has been inspired by both his love for the desert and a long struggle with chronic pain. He writes, "It is my wish that everyone who experiences chronic pain can find a little beauty in their struggle, and the inspiration to progress toward their dreams."

This is Joshua's second book of photos. His first, *Peace in the Paroxysm*, featured both photos and musings.

Joshua can be found on Instagram.

www.instagram.com/JoshuaPettitPhotography

www.ingramcontent.com/pod-product-compliance
Lightning Source LLC
Chambersburg PA
CBHW040045240726

48664CB00004B/1072